At Home in the
Heart of the Horseshoe

At Home in the Heart of the Horseshoe

Life in the

UNIVERSITY OF SOUTH CAROLINA PRESIDENT'S HOUSE

Patricia Moore-Pastides

FOREWORD BY HARRIS PASTIDES

THE UNIVERSITY OF SOUTH CAROLINA PRESS

© 2017 University of South Carolina

Published by the University of South Carolina Press
Columbia, South Carolina 29208

www.sc.edu/uscpress

Manufactured in China

26 25 24 23 22 21 20 19 18 17 10 9 8 7 6 5 4 3 2 1

Library of Congress Cataloging-in-Publication Data
can be found at http://catalog.loc.gov/.

ISBN: 978-1-61117-780-0 (cloth)
ISBN: 978-1-61117-781-7 (ebook)

"Help Me to Believe in Beginnings": From *Guerrillas of Grace* ©
Ted Loder, admin. Augsburg Fortress. Reproduced by permission.

"The Irresistible Ones": Reprinted by permission of Nikky Finney.

"Psalm for the Dying": Excerpted from *Prayers for a Planetary Pilgrim*
by Edward M. Hays, © 1989, 2008. Used with the permission of the
publisher, Forest of Peace, an imprint of Ave Maria Press®, Inc., Notre
Dame, Indiana, 46556. www.forestofpeace.com.

Frontispiece: First Lady Patricia Moore-Pastides and President
Harris Pastides at the door of the President's House.
PHOTOGRAPH BY KEITH MCGRAW.

All author royalties will be donated to the University of South Carolina.

To Harris, Katharine, and Andrew:
"Home" will always be wherever we are
whenever we're together.

Contents

PART ONE. The House and First Families of the Past

PART TWO. The House and First Family Today

PART THREE. Entertainment Ideas for Your House

Foreword — *Harris Pastides*

On the evening of July 31, 2008, just hours before I began my first full day as the twenty-eighth president of the University of South Carolina, Patricia and I drove to the back entrance of the historic President's House and quietly slipped inside.

After a restless sleep, we arose early to walk the 167 steps across the shaded Horseshoe to my new office in the Osborne Administration Building. And even though I would travel this same route thousands of times in the years ahead, there was something magical about emerging from the front door of the magnificent President's House on that morning.

Much has been written about the relationship between a president and his or her university. Many of the comments have become clichéd—"It's not a job, it's an obsession," or "A president's life is a 24/7 commitment." One of the funniest quips defines a university president as someone who lives in a mansion but is always begging for money! Far less has been written about the meaning and impact of actually living in the President's House, particularly a house located in the very heart of a flagship university.

Patricia has succeeded in rendering this house a home and has brought its former residents to life in this wonderfully approachable book. And even though I live in the house, I freely admit that, through Patricia's colorful recounting, I have become reacquainted with its rich history and better understand our great good fortune to be its residents.

Patricia makes many other essential contributions to our cherished university. As a public-health professional, she provides a clarion voice for good nutrition, helping our students, faculty, staff, and guests make healthier dietary choices. For example many of the advances we have made regarding healthier selections in our dining halls, on-campus restaurants, and catered special events began with Patricia's leadership. A goal of hers has been for the University of South Carolina to be recognized as one of the top ten food universities in America. In The Daily Meal website ratings of the 75 Best Colleges for Food in 2015, USC was ranked for the first time at number twenty-three. The Daily Meal rates universities on nutrition and sustainability, accessibility and service, education and events, the surrounding area, and the "x" factor—the little extras that prove the university goes above and beyond and is genuinely creative. She believes our first-ever ranking positioned us well to achieve the top ten during our tenure. In 2016 we earned twenty-first place, so we're on our way.

Patricia's books, *Greek Revival: Cooking for Life* and *Greek Revival from the Garden: Growing and Cooking for Life,* focus on Mediterranean customs and diet and continue to be big sellers for the University of South Carolina Press. Her books connect her efforts with groups well beyond the University of South Carolina community, and thus she brings our university acclaim.

She takes an active role in Healthy Carolina's initiatives to "make the healthy choice, the easy choice on campus." She offers a President's House table where tastes of garden produce are featured at the Healthy Carolina Farmers Market. She's actively engaged with the Gamecocks Live Well initiative to encourage daily exercise. She promotes lactation lounges and lactation support for new mothers in our community, and she's a fervent advocate for Tobacco Free Carolina.

Patricia has also been a moving force behind Carolina's sustainability efforts. The harvest of this work can be seen in the raised-bed gardens tended on campus, as well as rain barrels, a greenhouse, and other energy conserving technologies.

Her efforts as one small part of Sustainable Carolina, a university-wide approach to living and teaching sustainability, have not gone unnoticed. USC has been awarded a gold STARS rating ("STARS" standing for "Sustainability Tracking, Assessment and Rating System"), a bronze Bike Friendly University award, and recognition from the Tree Campus USA program of the Arbor Day Foundation.

Patricia has contributed to all this while continuing to uphold the well-established and far-reaching traditions of hospitality and entertaining that have become the trademark of the role of First Lady at USC. Her warmth shines through her events small and large and touches thousands of colleagues and visitors each year.

Together we've kept the traditions of the house alive by hosting more than thirty-five thousand visitors. While our door has opened to government leaders, entertainers, and other celebrities, the memories that we will cherish the most are the visits from our students and their families. I'll remember a small gathering of students seated in a circle in the stately library, chatting informally while they gazed at the leather-bound volumes, marveled at furniture crafted in another era, or admired nineteenth-century paintings hung near modern sculpture. We have always believed that this is their home away from home.

And it's not always quiet or stately. On the night before ESPN's "GameDays on the Shoe," hundreds of students bring tents and camp out on the Horseshoe. The festive mood is celebratory and contagious. There will be little sleep at the President's House anyway, so Patricia and I open our doors and float among our neighbors. She delivers healthy snacks as I'm talking football, "high-fiving," and taking selfies.

A particularly special memory from the President's House occurred during the "great blizzard" of February 2013, when an impressive, if modest, blanket of snow covered the Horseshoe. As the city came to a standstill and classes were cancelled for the next day, the Horseshoe became ground zero for raucous snowball fights. When a second day brought more closures, I decided to tweet out a message inviting students for a tour of the President's House. This is what I discovered: if you ask them, they will come . . . in droves! It will be one of the sweetest memories of my presidency.

On that first day at Osborne, Board Secretary Tommy Stepp opened his remarks with, "When South Carolina College was founded in 1801, Thomas Jefferson was the third president of the United States." Thomas Jefferson had in fact encouraged the establishment of this fine university. With Mr. Stepp's statement, Patricia and I felt a distinct thrill, realizing that we would become part of the legacy of such a historic institution. Not unlike other presidents and their spouses, we've attempted to approach our positions with openness toward the entire university community. This attitude has resulted in the gift of rich and full lives for us.

Life in the President's House situates us at the heart of USC and as the inheritors of the finest legacies and traditions of former first families. I know you will enjoy reading about their contributions as we recognize, honor, and appreciate the role of First Ladies in the warm and welcoming culture that is the trademark of the University of South Carolina.

Preface

In May 2009 Harris and I had the pleasure of visiting the University of Virginia and having lunch with then-president John Casteen and his wife, Betsy. President Casteen had been in office for nearly twenty years, so we enjoyed his perspective and listened intently as he shared lessons learned during his long tenure. At the conclusion of our visit, Betsy gave me a beautiful coffee-table book called *Carr's Hill*, which is the name of the President's House at Virginia. I immediately considered compiling a comparable book to showcase the President's House at the University of South Carolina. I thought it would make a beautiful gift for our guests and a wonderful keepsake for our 282,000 alumni worldwide. And while literally thousands of people—students, faculty, staff, alumni, donors, honorary-degree recipients, dignitaries, and other special guests—visit the President's House each year, I meet people regularly who have never been here, and I expected they might enjoy a peek inside the historic property as well.

Knowing that the University of South Carolina Press takes great care to ensure their books are artful, I proposed a colorful book that could represent the magnificent home and gardens on the historic Horseshoe. And because of the university's tradition of entertaining, I knew I wanted to include some favored recipes as well as ideas for creative floral arrangements and holiday decorations.

While I appreciate beauty and food, I knew that taking a "home and garden" approach would not sufficiently honor the historic relevance of this place. I felt compelled to write about some of the noteworthy people who have visited the house and the meaningful events that have enlivened it. And because I'm often asked, "What's it like to live there?" I wanted to write about daily life in the house. On the other hand, I was certain that I *didn't* want to write about the legacies of the presidents. I've left that work for the true historians.

As my mission evolved, I felt the book would be most interesting if it included personal stories and cherished memories from previous First Ladies and family members who inhabited the house. This task was quite manageable because the current President's House became exclusively the residence of the president's family in 1952. Therefore it was possible to contact relatives of six of the seven presidents who have lived here since then.

In the spirit of southern oral tradition, I thought it would be great fun to ask family members of the presidents what they remember about life on the Horseshoe, both within the home and on campus. Indeed it was! The stories woven into these pages were told to me by children, spouses, and one grandchild of USC presidents. I think you will enjoy these tales as much as I did and find that they open a window into life in the President's House.

In addition to others' stories, I combed through hundreds of events that we've hosted and selected several that are especially significant to share with you.

The USC President's House holds memories for thousands of people, and its many visitors have created vibrant tales. *At Home in the Heart of the Horseshoe: Life in the University of South Carolina President's House* invites you to enjoy handsome architecture, exquisite antiques, well-appointed rooms, great recipes, easy decorating tips, glorious gardens, meaningful historic events, and the *just plain living* that has taken place in this home.

I hope you enjoy your visit to the President's House in these pages.

Acknowledgments

Karen Rood, editor. Though officially retired from the USC Press, Karen worked me into her vigorous travel schedule. This was the deal I made with the USC Press director early on, as Karen edited my previous books, and I knew I wanted her for this one. She has a sharp mind for organization and detail, and we have a rapport that promotes authenticity. In other words she tells me gently when I'm sounding cheesy. Spending a few hours with Karen ensures lunch, and she doesn't mind having only vegetables. Books brought us together, but food made us friends.

Lisa Robinette, President's House manager, assistant director of special events, and in the case of this book, manager of photography. This type of work is painstakingly slow, and Lisa voluntarily worked several late nights until she was satisfied that every photograph we used was a high-quality picture. We photograph nearly all presidential events at USC, consequently the photo galleries are vast. Lisa helped hone those into manageable categories so we could make selections. She then created a numbering system for the hundreds of photographs we chose and spent hours carefully keying them to the text. Over time we replaced many of the original choices with more recent or clearer ones, and Lisa managed the substitutions. Thank you, Lisa.

In addition to being proficient at all she does, Lisa truly loves the President's House and cares for it as if it were her own. Despite hours and days of assiduous, taxing work, she joined me for some tear-filled laughs as we recounted stories from residents of this ostensibly distinguished house.

Lisa and Pam Bowman, who directs special events at USC, are my promoters, marketing team, protectors, and confidantes. They also manage my schedule. Their support allows me to be actively engaged with our community. Without them I could accomplish very little, and with them I am reminded to breathe. Any university presidential spouse who feels overwhelmed by their role does not have a team like Pam and Lisa, and while I may pity those spouses, I'm not sharing!

Lisa and Pam currently work with a staff of four: Betsy Suddeth, Alysha Battaglia, Ryan Fanning Reed, and Meagan Crowl. They also employ student intern Kailey Gregrow, a history major. I really cannot emphasize how much they accomplish for USC, where special events are an elaborate tradition.

While I'm thanking people who support me, allow me to mention Joyce Taylor, the President's House housekeeper. Joyce is a dedicated employee as well as a close member of our "work family." Sharon Williams works with Joyce part-time to help put the house back together after events.

Horticulturist Charlie Ryan makes many of the magnificent floral arrangements for the house, including those adorning the front doors. He and his team, currently David Robbins and students Sarah Sprague, Phil Hust, and Sonna Boothroyd do an amazing job in the botanical and vegetable gardens as well as on the Horseshoe and behind Russell House (our student center), where they cultivate our community herb garden.

I work very closely with David Sauers, resident district manager of Sodexo at USC. He has done an amazing job to expand food choices and to create a fabulous team of chefs and catering managers. He cares deeply about environmental sustainability and the health of our diners. Dave serves as a member of the Healthy Carolina advisory board, whose mission is to make the healthy choice the easy choice on campus. Dave was generous in offering the time and talents of then-presidential chef Blake Clevenger and presidential catering manager Don Staley as expert contributors to this work.

Amie Ritner, now retired from the university, was called in an emergency to help with holiday decorations after one of our staff members had an accident. In the designer's absence, she executed the "Green Present" with aplomb (see p. 149). I want to thank Jonathan Haupt, former director of USC Press, for his support of this project. He respected my wish to include many aspects of life in the house, even though we initially struggled with how to encompass it all in one book. I have the distinct impression that he hand-picked outside readers who would think like me. In any case, I appreciate the USC Press taking this on. And as always, the production value of *At Home in the Heart of the Horseshoe* is laudable, which a 163-year-old historic home deserves. I wish to acknowledge and thank Pat Callahan, head of the USC Press design and production department, for her fine work.

Kevin Millham, another person with serious organizational skills, indexed this book. He is thorough and conscientious. He also has a great sense of humor. In the spring of 2016 I asked him to hold time in February 2017. Here is his reply: "Nice to hear from you again! Sure, I'll hold the time with advance notice like this—just hope I'm still above the ground a year from now." A great guy, Kevin meticulously imagines all the ways a reader would use an index. Neuroscientists would assure me that editing his index serves to grow my brain, and I've discovered such a gain is more like a hearty game of Scrabble—really fun and not intolerably painful.

Keith McGraw and Jason Ayer shot most of the current photographs during presidential events, and Phil Sawyer, who has since retired from the university, was responsible for many of the photographs from previous administrations. Kim Truett, who works in the Office of Communications and Public Affairs, also contributed photographs to this book. I thank each photographer for their contributions. A book such as this one requires lovely stills of the house and gardens and fun-filled photographs of people enjoying them. Thanks to our contributing photographers, we can call this mission accomplished.

I wish to offer my sincere gratitude to Nikky Finney for granting me permission to reprint "The Irresistible Ones," a powerful commemorative poem about the three brave students who desegregated the University of South Carolina in 1963. My gratitude for her presence on our campus and in our state is ever renewed by her work, which continually challenges us to understand each other more fully. Ms. Finney was awarded the National Book Award for Poetry in 2011 for *Head Off and Split,* and she holds the John H. Bennett, Jr., Chair in Creative Writing and Southern Letters at the University of South Carolina.

Ronald D. Long from Charlton Hall Galleries, Inc., assisted me in describing significant furnishings in the President's House. Ron alerted me to some previously unrecognized gems and at least one reproduction masquerading as an original.

We were extremely fortunate to have Peter Kenney, a longtime curator and administrator of the American Wing of the Metropolitan Museum, and Margize Howell, who served as curator, director of development, and executive director of Classical American Homes, visit the USC President's House in the summer of 2016. Mr. Kenney and Ms. Howell are currently copresidents of Classical American Homes and were visiting our library collections with Dean Tom McNally. They took time from their schedule on campus to tour the President's House and share their insights on the furnishings. We are appreciative of their time and expertise and sincerely hope this was the first of many future visits and a long friendship.

I would like to thank Dean of Libraries Tom McNally and his team, especially Beth Bilderback and Craig Keeney of the South Caroliniana Library, who—with Elizabeth Sudduth, director of the Irvin Department of Rare Books and Special Collections and the Ernest F. Hollings Special Collections Library at the Thomas Cooper Library, and Herb Hartsook, director of the South Carolina Political Collections in that same library—assisted with documentation describing the maps and paintings that are holdings of the university libraries.

Jane Przybysz, executive director of McKissick Museum and her staff, especially Mark Smith, curator for Exhibition and Collection Management, contributed to the explanations of the holdings of the museum that are displayed at the President's House.

Elizabeth Cassidy West, university archivist, read the manuscript for historical accuracy and differentiated legend from fact in a few instances. I thank her and her team for their invaluable contributions and sleuthing out archival photographs and documents. History professor Bobby Donaldson was especially helpful in sharing his knowledge of university history.

Eleanor Swarat, director of Planned Giving, and Lindsey Fisher of University Foundations were helpful in verifying the provenance of much of the furniture in the President's House.

I wish to thank all those who've taken an interest in documenting the history and furnishings of the President's House, including former house staffers and managers Ora Lee Danzler, Carol Lund, Carol Benfield, Lori Miles, Gloria Bauknight, Jean Weingarth, and Barbara Riddle Caston.

In "The University of South Carolina's Historic President's House" (*Columbia Metropolitan,* January-February 1992), J. Cantey Heath Jr., currently secretary of the University and Board of Trustees, provided an insightful history alive with the antics of children and university students. He reinforced my vision to shed light on the living that takes place in the house.

Notes left by George Terry, vice provost and dean of libraries (1991–2001), for his own work on the President's House were an inspiration to this project. I always felt a special connection to Dr. Terry, who chaired the search committee that brought us to South Carolina in 1998. Just around the time of his passing, I had asked him to present a preview of his book at a University Women's Club meeting. While that presentation never occurred, I hope to give many in his honor over the coming years.

Answering the questions "What do you remember most about campus life?" and "What was your life like when you lived in the President's House?" were the stars of *At Home in the Heart of the Horseshoe:* Donald Russell, Cissie Snow, Elizabeth Sumwalt Clark, Elizabeth Bradley, Nancy Smith, Jamie Hall, Norma Palms, and Donna Sorensen. Though unable to answer those same exact questions, colleagues of President and Mrs. William H. Patterson, the late Harold Brunton and Keith Davis, provided insight into the Pattersons' time in the home. And Carl "Billy" Watson (B.S. 1955, J.D. 1958), who was president of his freshman class and served on student council during the Russell administration, shared his memories of Mrs. Russell, particularly her influence on campus. He generously donated his invitation to Senior Dinner to the project.

Hearing the memories and family tales from each of the interviewees was by far and away the highlight of this work for me. I sincerely appreciate the alacrity with which my subjects shared their experiences on campus and at home on the Horseshoe. Their stories brought this book to life and made this house a home.

PART ONE

The House and
First Families of the Past

The original President's House, circa 1910. UNIVERSITY ARCHIVES.

The Original President's House

The first President's House on campus was located at the top of the historic Horseshoe, where the McKissick Museum stands today. It was a two-story brick building, completed in 1807 for eight thousand dollars. Jonathan Maxcy, the first university president (1804–1820), lived off campus with his wife, Susanna Hopkins Maxcy, and family until the residence was finished. They then resided in the President's House throughout the rest of President Maxcy's tenure, which ended with his untimely death at the age of fifty-two in 1820.

The building survived two earthquakes, one in 1811 and the other in 1886. In 1849 the house was updated with running water. The building was repaired in 1856, and front and rear porches were added. And in 1857 gas lines were installed.

Students were boisterous in the early years of South Carolina College. Various practical jokes—such as sneaking

President William Howard Taft speaking from the porch of the original President's House, 1909.
UNIVERSITY ARCHIVES.

3

behind the house to paint the president's horse an "unnatural color"—and even student demonstrations were not rare.

In one instance students burned an effigy of a professor while President Maxcy pleaded for order. The professor, George Blackburn, had reported students trying to steal the college bell. In retaliation a large cohort of students not only burned his effigy but broke into DeSaussure College on campus, ransacked the library, and stole the bell anyway. The local militia had to be called to restore control.

In 1862, during the Civil War, the college closed, and the Confederate Army used most campus buildings as a hospital. The original President's House, left vacant in 1862 and 1863, was then rented until 1865, when it became an officers' hospital.

When the college reopened as the University of South Carolina in 1865, it did not have a president but rather a chairman of the faculty. From then until 1873, the President's House became a faculty residence. In that year the state legislature created a normal school for the training of schoolteachers, which was open to both black and white students. Even though the school was not formally part of the University of South Carolina, some of the courses were taught at the President's House.

From the conclusion of the Civil War until 1877 the university was the only one in the South to operate in an integrated fashion, including African American students, faculty, and trustees. In 1877 it closed its doors until 1880, when it reopened as the whites-only South Carolina College of Agriculture and Mechanics. During the time the university was closed, the President's House was rented to private individuals. When the school reopened, the house became the president's residence once again and so it remained for forty-two years. Though the university reorganized and changed names again, the house continued as the president's residence until William D. Melton was named president in 1922 and decided to remain in his private Columbia home, rather than move into the official President's House. At that time the house was converted into university offices, including the registrar's office, the personnel bureau, graduate and alumni offices, the dean of women's office, and the university's news service.

In the early 1930s the building was condemned. As plans to build what was later named the McKissick Library were developed, it was first suggested that the home could be relocated, but in 1939 that plan was deemed unfeasible and the original President's House was demolished.

Two views of the original President's House, circa 1920. UNIVERSITY ARCHIVES.

The original Presient's House, circa 1930, when it was used as USC offices. UNIVERSITY ARCHIVES.

Demolition of the original President's House in front of the newly constructed library (now McKissick Museum). UNIVERSITY ARCHIVES.

The History of the Building
We Now Call the President's House

The home that we know as the President's House today was built as faculty housing in 1854. A regency-style duplex, it was designed to accommodate two families. Building the house cost eleven thousand dollars, and it was considered "a great improvement on the plan and style of the college residencies" (Edwin L. Green, *History of the Buildings of the University of South Carolina,* 1909). It had thirteen fireplaces and high ceilings.

Some of the notable faculty who resided here were chemistry professor William B. Burney, who taught at the university for more than fifty years, and Dr. George Armstrong Wauchope, an English professor who wrote the lyrics to the alma mater in 1911.

J. Rion McKissick and his wife, Caroline Dick McKissick, moved into the house in 1931 when he was dean of the School of Journalism. He then became the first president to live here when he was elected president in 1936. He remained in the house until his death in 1944.

Between President McKissick's tenure and the residence being converted to the official President's House in 1952, the building was used as a women's dorm and was shared by two sororities, Alpha Delta Pi and Pi Beta Phi. Both moved to Sims College on campus in 1949. For a time part of the property was used for the university radio station. During the years 1945–1952, university presidents lived in their own private homes near campus.

President J. Rion McKissick and Mrs. Caroline McKissick dancing, 1940. UNIVERSITY ARCHIVES.

HISTORIC USES OF THE
CURRENT PRESIDENT'S HOUSE BUILDING

1854	The regency-style duplex is opened as a residence for two faculty families.
1865	Trinity Episcopal Church rents the east side for a brief time.
1883–1930	Chemistry professor William B. Burney resides in the east side of the house for forty-seven of the fifty-one years he teaches at the University of South Carolina.
1903–1943	English professor George A. Wauchope, author of the lyrics to "We Hail Thee Carolina," resides in the west side of the house. By the early 1900s the house is known as the Wauchope House.
1931–1944	Dean of Journalism J. Rion McKissick moves into the east side of the house. He continues living there after becoming university president in 1936, remaining until his death in 1944.
1944–1949	The residence serves as women's housing.
1949–1952	The house is vacant and in need of repair.

Source: Elizabeth Cassidy West and Katharine Thompson Allen, *On the Horseshoe: A Guide to the Historic Campus of the University of South Carolina* (Columbia: University of South Carolina Press, 2015).

An 1875 photograph of the faculty duplex that became the President's House in 1952.
UNIVERSITY ARCHIVES.

Two views of the front of the President's House before the 1970s renovation project, when parking was still allowed on the Horseshoe and the fountain was still in front of the house. UNIVERSITY ARCHIVES.

The President's House after the renovations, probably late 1970s or early 1980s. UNIVERSITY ARCHIVES.

The fountain in front of the President's House before it was moved to the back garden in the mid-1970s. UNIVERSITY ARCHIVES.

The President's House at Christmas in the 1980s after the fountain was moved. UNIVERSITY ARCHIVES.

The President's House in the 1990s. UNIVERSITY ARCHIVES.

First Families Who Resided in the Current President's House

Since 1952 eight families have lived in the President's House. I have the pleasure of sharing some of their memories here.

❧ 1952–1957: The Russell Family

The twenty-first president, Donald S. Russell, and his wife, Virginia Utsey Russell, converted the house into the single-family President's House, where their family of six was the first to reside. Their children are Donald, Mildred, Scott, and John.

The Russells moved from Spartanburg when he assumed the presidency of the University of South Carolina in 1952. President Russell did not accept a salary, and he and Mrs. Russell took it upon themselves to renovate the somewhat run-down duplex, which at that point had become known as the McKissick-Wauchope House, into the beautiful single-family President's House.

The Russells' eldest child, Donald Jr., resided in the President's House from the middle of his junior year at University High School until his junior year at the University of South Carolina, when he moved into an apartment with some fraternity brothers. I enjoyed hearing Donald talk about life in the President's House. One of his earliest memories is of the university treasurer visiting his father in the house and asking if he was aware of the amount of money Mrs. Russell was spending on the renovation. President Russell admitted he was not but added, "I suppose we should pay for that too."

To accommodate their massive book collection, Mrs. Russell had bookcases built that covered all the walls of the living room. Even though some of them have since been covered with paneling, we still refer to the room as the library.

Adjacent to the library, the front dining room was used for formal dinners, and the back dining room was for family meals.

Mrs. Russell hired the foremost American interior designer of the day, William Pahlmann, to find beautiful pieces for the house. Probably the most spectacular is the wallcovering in the reception room on the second floor. In a pattern known as Procession Chinoise, the wallcovering dates back to approximately 1811 and was made in France. Because of its age, its exact provenance is difficult to trace, but Donald remembers his parents' declaration that it was "extraordinarily select." Depicting a European fantasy of a Chinese wedding scene, the wallpaper was made by block printing, a process in which a series of carved wood blocks were inked and pressed onto paper, which was then applied to a fabric backing.

When Donald Jr.'s fraternity moved into the fraternity section of McBryde Quad, Mrs. Russell sent Mr. Pahlmann to consult on the décor and purchase furnishings for the fraternity house as well. That frat was certainly in good company.

As Donald recalls, panty raids were common in the springtime. It seems women living in the Women's Quad would throw their panties out the windows to young men waiting below. One night the USC police came to the President's House to request President Russell's intervention to break up a large crowd of male students who had congregated at the Women's Quad to participate in one such event. Donald remembers his father wearing a pair of slacks and a bathrobe and heading out to address the throng of students. Recognizing a few football players and eliciting their assistance, President Russell urged the young men to return to their dorms, and they did. I recounted this story to Mr. and

President and Mrs. Russell greeting guests in the library. Also in the receiving line are Joseph Norwood, dean of the College of Arts and Sciences; Arney Childs, dean of women; Captain W. L. Anderson, head of Naval Sciences, and Mrs. Anderson. UNIVERSITY ARCHIVES.

President and Mrs. Russell dining with their four children (clockwise from President Russell's left): Mildred, Scott, John, and Donald. UNIVERSITY ARCHIVES.

Mrs. Bob McNair during their recent visit to campus. Mr. McNair remembers that evening well. To rally the troops, one of his fraternity brothers played a trumpet with a pair of ladies panties hanging from it!

When the Russells first moved into the President's House, the garden comprised nothing but dirt and soot from the smokestack behind the house. It was the perfect sand pile for the younger children, who loved to dig in the yard. Once their archaeological finds were weight plates, which Donald confiscated, cleaned up, and stuck on a broom handle. This was the start of his interest in bodybuilding. He proceeded to buy more weights from Todd and Moore Sporting Goods, whose weight department he claims to have subsidized as he pursued the goal of becoming a Muscle Beach body-builder.

President Russell hired Warren Giese as football coach. One evening while President and Mrs. Russell were entertaining Mr. Giese in the library, the coach became distracted by noises upstairs and asked if there was work being done. President and Mrs. Russell recognized the familiar sounds of Donald's weight lifting and told Mr. Giese, it was just their teenage son bound for Muscle Beach. Mr. Giese became agitated, telling the Russells that this was the worst thing for a teenage boy, that lifting weights would cause his heart to become enlarged, and that he would lose flexibility. Despite Mr. Giese's strong opinion, Donald remained undeterred.

As for his experience living in the President's House as a USC student, Donald shared that his parents usually did not involve themselves with his academic life. He was a good student who made Phi Beta Kappa as a sophomore. In his day good students had unlimited "cuts" from classes, but from time to time President Russell would see Donald's professors on the Horseshoe, and they would "snitch" on him. Donald remembers one morning when his father called the house to rouse him because one of his professors had just informed his father that he wasn't coming to class.

Of the many renowned guests Donald remembers his family entertaining at the President's House, Senator John F. Kennedy was the most distinguished. Before his visit, when Mrs. Russell graciously asked the senator if there was anything she could do to make his stay more comfortable, Senator Kennedy, who had a bad back, asked if she would have a board placed under the mattress of the bed he was to sleep on. Mrs. Russell tested various thicknesses of plywood and finally settled on a ¾-inch piece. The morning after the senator's stay, however, she learned from the housekeeper that

Senator John F. Kennedy speaking at University of South Carolina commencement, May 31, 1957. UNIVERSITY ARCHIVES.

her efforts had been for naught. All the bedding was found on the floor; the senator had not slept on the bed after all.

Donald believes that the most memorable events for students during the Russell administration were the senior-class dinners. After beautifying the garden, Mrs. Russell hosted dinners for all members of the senior class in groups of approximately one hundred. She set up long tables and worked with the housekeeper and the housekeeper's husband in the kitchen to prepare the food, and she hired several waiters to serve it. Mrs. Russell loved to cook. Donald said she had a large bookcase with six or seven shelves of cookbooks. Both he and his classmate Carl "Billy" Watson remember his mother serving fried chicken, corn, macaroni and cheese, and green beans. Others remember Mrs. Russell's Country Captain over rice. But regardless of the entrée, the dessert was the highlight. Donald unequivocally praises his mother's strawberry shortcake as legendary. He recounts that she had two large cooking pots filled with strawberries for the dessert, one puréed and the other sliced. She made large homemade biscuits, better than any Donald has had anywhere, even in fine restaurants. She topped the biscuits with strawberry purée and sliced strawberries, and crowned the dessert with real whipped cream.

I spoke to Billy Watson as I was particularly interested in learning more about the Senior Dinner, and found that Mrs. Russell had many positive influences within the university community. Not only were her Senior Dinners warm affairs, where Mrs. Russell herself helped to serve and clear and took the opportunity to chat with the students, but she urged students to offer their suggestions to her and the president. Billy and other members of student government shared their distress and disbelief that administrators planned to tear down McCutchen House on the Horseshoe and build a modern student union. Billy attributed the saving of McCutchen House to Mrs. Russell.

Billy also shared how Mrs. Russell supervised the planting and watering of oaks on the Horseshoe, which prompted him and his classmates to muse, "Only God and Mrs. Russell can make a tree."

Mrs. Russell was steadfast in her commitment that every student would have dinner at the President's House before they graduated. How magnanimous she was! I love the idea, but with 7,786 seniors, I'd have to start in September, and it would be a bit like painting the Golden Gate Bridge! I believe that her beautiful spirit of entertaining set the tone for the traditions we hold dear today, and the warm culture of this university.

One issue that will always be with us is the uncertainty of the weather when planning garden events. Mrs. Russell relied on the Farmers' Almanac in the fall to choose Senior Dinner dates in May. As Donald fondly reminisces, "It never rained on Mother's Senior Dinners."

Mrs. Russell serving fried chicken at a Senior Dinner. UNIVERSITY ARCHIVES.

Students attending the Russells' Senior Dinner. UNIVERSITY ARCHIVES.

President and Mrs. Donald Russell
cordially invite you
to the
Senior Dinner
6:30 Friday evening, April 29, 1955
The President's Home
R.S.V.P. Informal

Invitation to Senior Dinner, 1955. COURTESY OF CARL "BILLY" WATSON.

President Robert Sumwalt (seated to the right of the lamp) and Mrs. Caroline Sumwalt (seated to the left of lamp) with their extended family in the President's House library. Granddaughter Elizabeth is seated on the table. UNIVERSITY ARCHIVES.

❧ 1957–1962: The Sumwalt Family

The President's House was next home to the twenty-second president, Robert L. Sumwalt, and his wife, Caroline Causey Sumwalt. When President Russell stepped down to run for governor of South Carolina, Dr. Robert Sumwalt was appointed acting president of the university and served in that capacity from 1957 until 1959. He was then named president and remained so until 1962.

Prior to becoming university president, Dr. Sumwalt was dean of the School of Engineering. President and Mrs. Sumwalt had a son, Bobby, who was already married with children at the time his parents resided in the President's House, so Bobby never lived here. President Sumwalt's granddaughter Elizabeth Sumwalt Clark has fond memories of spending time at the President's House and was happy to share some of them.

Elizabeth, who called her grandparents "Bob" and "Nine," remembers coming into town frequently as a child and freely roaming the Horseshoe. She recalls a group of freshmen boys wearing beanies and singing in the President's House garden, as well as a Christmas caroling party in the ballroom on the second floor, where faculty and students sang from books of carols. She loved to dance all around the large ballroom when it was unoccupied. Elizabeth also recalls formal events on the Horseshoe in the spring to celebrate Derby Day and May Day. She and her brother are depicted as adorable members of the May Court in the 1962 *Garnet and Black* yearbook.

Elizabeth recounted the following cherished memory of the day her Brownie Scout troop met at the USC President's House:

1961—The Brownie Scout Meeting in Elizabeth's Own Words

It was a proud day for me when I hosted my Brownie Troop from Trinity Episcopal Church (now Trinity Cathedral) for a meeting at the President's House in approximately 1961. My grandparents, "Nine and Bob" Sumwalt, lived in the house while he was President of the University. I was thrilled to be able to host my Brownie friends and wanted it to be perfect. My mother and grandmother helped me plan the meeting, and I wrote out the agenda in my diary:

Brownie Meeting
1. Get here
2. Play
3. Eat (cheese crackers and brownies and Coke)
4. See house
5. Go to Bob's office
6. Come back and play

We assembled in the spacious living room and then adjourned to the formal dining room, where Margie Waymer, my grandparents' cook who worked for them for many, many years, served us a lovely snack (cheese crackers, brownies, and Cokes, and probably her delicious butterscotch brownies and petits fours). I imagine that Nine conducted the tour of the house, up one stairway, into the beautiful ballroom, through the 2nd and 3rd floor bedrooms and family living quarters, and down the opposite stairway. It seemed like a mansion to me!

After touring the house, it was time to walk across the Horseshoe to the Administration Building to visit Bob in his office. Imagine the sight for the students to see eleven little Brownie Scouts scampering across the Horseshoe! They must have had a laugh! Bob loved children and made us feel so comfortable in his formal office. He arranged to have a photographer take our picture assembled around him in his office chair. There I was, seated at his feet with a proud smile on my face and with a red ribbon tied around my neck securing my diary key. I had a lot to write about that night!

I'm sure there were times when President and Mrs. Sumwalt called their son to retrieve the children, including the time Elizabeth and a friend hurled water balloons from a third floor bedroom window near students walking below. Elizabeth doesn't remember any direct hits, just several surprised looks from students being water bombed.

President Sumwalt with Elizabeth's Brownie Scout troop, 1961. *Seated:* Sally Eggleston, Hayden Dibble, Elizabeth Sumwalt, Jane Tucker Dana, Mary Murray Black. *Standing:* Beth Williams, Kitty Kelly, Alice Barron Pearce, Frances Weston, Sally Clarkson, and Betsy Baesel. COURTESY OF ELIZABETH CLARK.

President Jones, Andrew, Jonathan, Katherine, Mrs. Mary Butterworth Jones, James, and Thomas in the President's House library, 1962. UNIVERSITY ARCHIVES.

❧ 1962–1974: The Jones Family

The twenty-third president, Thomas F. Jones, his wife, Mary Butterworth Jones, and their five children—Thomas, James, Jonathan, Katherine (Cissie), and Andrew—were the third family to make their home in the President's House.

The Jones family moved to South Carolina from Indiana, where Dr. Jones had been dean of the Department of Electrical Engineering at Purdue University.

Of the five Jones children, Cissie was the only girl. Thomas was the eldest child, followed by Jim, Jonathan, Cissie, and Andy. I had the pleasure of interviewing Cissie, who shared a flood of memories during her first visit to her former home.

Cissie remembers arriving at the President's House for the first time in May 1962 as a seven year old. The Jones family

was met in the kitchen by a staff of six African American maids, cooks, and a butler/chauffeur. The maids wore uniforms of green button-down dresses, hose, and white shoes. The butler wore a starched white jacket. The family was not accustomed to having household help, and Cissie had never met an African American person in Indiana. She remembers asking Evelyn, one of the housekeepers, "Why are you brown?" She answered, "Because God made me that way."

The Jones family ate their meals in the back dining room, where President Jones had a call button under the rug near his foot to summon the staff. The Jones children often ate supper in the kitchen with the house staff when their parents ate later after events. As there was no kitchen in the family apartment on the second floor, the family usually called downstairs to order their breakfast, and it was brought upstairs to them.

Cissie remembers that in those days everyone smoked, including her parents and the maids while ironing.

Mrs. Jones was quite uncomfortable with having a houseful of servants. Caroline Sumwalt tried to mentor her but to no avail. "Mom had no personal assistant, her schedule was handled through Dad's office," says Cissie. "She was a little outspoken to begin with, and they had some parties with great debates. She would say just what she thought."

When they first moved into the President's House, the two older boys were assigned to bedrooms on the third floor. The younger three children shared a bedroom next to their parents' bedroom. The two boys had bunk beds, and Cissie had a single bed in the corner near the sun porch. The bedrooms now called the McKissick and Kennedy rooms were reserved for guests.

The Jones children were not allowed in the library or the front dining room except to pass through. Cissie claims that, as a child, she was "creeped out" by old portraits of former presidents, whose eyes seemed to follow her through the room. She learned to dart through the front rooms and jump three stairs at once to get upstairs as quickly as possible.

Strom Thurmond was a family friend. Her parents introduced Strom to his future wife Nancy. Their wedding reception in 1968 was held in the President's House ballroom on the second floor. Cissie poured punch.

By the start of Cissie's sophomore year of high school, public schools were desegregated in South Carolina. She had attended Dreher High School for her freshman year and was zoned into Booker T. Washington High School the following year. BTW had been an all-black school, and under the desegregation plan, it was to become 60 percent black and 40 percent white. With white flight, however, BTW comprised 80 percent black and 20 percent white students. Most of the Caucasian students at BTW were children of the mill workers in Olympia, and Cissie remembers them as "tough kids." At Thurmond's urging, Dr. and Mrs. Jones attempted to send Cissie to Ashley Hall in Charleston, but Cissie was determined to attend BTW. She loved playing basketball. She habitually arrived at school by 6:00 A.M. to practice basketball until school opened. As the only white player on the court, she earned the nickname "Spot."

Cissie said it was a privilege to attend BTW. The teachers

The Booker T. Washington class of 1973. Cissie Jones is the girl with the short blonde hair first row standing third from left. COURTESY OF BOBBY DONALDSON.

were a combination of older folks and young hippies. She and her friends had a penchant for getting into trouble for fun. They would start fake riots to get out of school, when in fact they were close friends. She credits Mrs. Fanny Phelps Adams and Coach Samuel Goodwin for guiding her and keeping her out of trouble—more or less.

University expansion resulted in the closing of BTW in 1974 as well as the destruction of neighborhoods surrounding the campus. The area where the Coliseum stands today was a neighborhood of "shotgun houses." When the buildings were razed, great numbers of dogs and cats were abandoned. Many of these strays ended up on campus in Cissie's care.

After graduating from BTW High School, Cissie attended Furman University for one year, and then transferred to USC, where she spent the next four years, graduating in 1978. She began her college career at USC as a basketball player and worked at Coach Frank McGuire's camp, but she ended up on the tennis team.

The President's House Menagerie

When she was thirteen, Cissie had a horse named Bali Hai, which she kept at Palmetto Downs racetrack at the state fairgrounds. She once rode the horse to the President's House, and kept her there overnight. The gardener was not happy the next day.

The original slave quarters behind the President's House had been used as the campus radio station, but it became Cissie's kennel for stray animals. She took care of them and found them homes. She had two special dogs that she kept as pets, Critter and Critter's husband. At one point they were relocated to Sesquicentennial State Park, but Critter found her way back. Quite pregnant on her return, she had eight puppies on Cissie's bed. Cissie kept Critter and two of those puppies. Critter subsequently had another litter under the kitchen. "Neutering wasn't as common back then," Cissie commented.

Cissie also told me a great story that ended with Critter winning the heart of Loretta Lynn, who was a dinner guest at the President's House. The tables were set in the ballroom to create one long table running the length of the room. When the guests were all seated, the three youngest Jones children, all dressed up, were presented to everyone. Then they were taken to the second-floor family room for "lock down," meaning they had a babysitter. Jonathan, Cissie, and Andy turned the tables on the sitter and locked her in a room. Then they

headed out to crash the dinner party. Together with three or four dogs, the children crawled along under the tables. Cissie remembers admiring Loretta Lynn's husband's cowboy boots. The children got in trouble, but their punishment was mitigated by the fact that Loretta Lynn thought it was the "coolest thing ever" and fed Critter, who remained under the table.

Cissie was quite the animal lover. She raised Vida, a blue jay, from a tiny baby. Vida lived in the house, drinking from Mrs. Jones's glass and sipping from a silver creamer. At cocktail hour Mrs. Jones would remove her earrings and place them on an end table. Vida carried some away and dropped them on top of the valances above the library draperies. It wasn't until the draperies were removed for cleaning that the jewelry was discovered. The family also had a pigeon named Alfi. Cissie's idea was to rehabilitate all the animals to return them to the wild, but that didn't always work out.

They had a sparrow named Boris for two years and a special-needs parakeet named Jerry. Jerry, Boris, and Vida enjoyed going for joy rides in female guests' bouffant hairdos, which always created havoc in the house! Squirrels would come in through the family-room window on the second floor to eat Cromer's peanuts, which the children and Mrs. Jones left for them on top of the television set.

One year Cissie bought her father a gamecock named Rusty for Christmas. She had a garnet and black harness made for Rusty at Gerald's Shoe Shop in Five Points, so Rusty could be walked, and sometimes he was taken to football games on the leash. Cissie brought home chickens that lived around Palmetto Downs to be his "girlfriends," and they all lived in the house.

Two problems arose with having Rusty and the chickens. One was that it wasn't possible to teach them to use a litter box, but the dogs took care of cleaning up after them. The other problem was that the students in Legare complained about the rooster crowing, so the window in the second-floor bathroom, where the rooster was kept, had to remain closed.

Events on Campus

In 1963 USC desegregated. Cissie says the overall feeling in her home was tense. There was a lot of whispering but no overt protests and no burning crosses.

Anti–Vietnam War demonstrations were quite another thing. After Kent State, students protested on campus, and SDS (Students for a Democratic Society) became active. With some leaders from Chicago, students broke into

Osborne Administration building, toppled files, and burned records. The National Guard was called in. The *Daily Gamecock* called Mrs. Jones the "Lioness Protecting her Den" because she refused to leave the President's House even though it was the target of rocks and Molotov cocktails.

She instructed all the children to stay indoors at the back of the house, but Cissie went to one of the windows in the Koger room overlooking the antiwar protesters, who were walking from Osborne toward the Maxcy monument. From Sumter Street came the National Guard troops with guns, gas masks, and shields—also heading toward the monument. Students were throwing things at the house. When the National Guard fired tear gas into the crowd of students, they retreated, and Cissie had to close the window as the tear gas rose.

That is Cissie's most dramatic memory of activity on the Horseshoe, but she also remembers her father, wearing his pajamas, addressing a crowd of twelve to fifteen thousand disgruntled students from the ballroom window on the second floor after the decision was made to leave the ACC.

The more frivolous student activities Cissie remembers were panty raids, the leg-judging "Miss Venus contest," and the Maypole spring dance. She also remembers a fraternity hazing that led to a couple of drunk, naked men on the third floor of the President's House!

Life in the House

"Mom loved Christmas!" says Cissie. Mrs. Jones had several Christmas trees throughout the house, garlands on the bannisters, and mantelpiece arrangements. She invited the student body to come caroling, providing songbooks and candles. After singing they were invited in to wander through the public rooms enjoying hot chocolate, eggnog, cookies, and petits fours. The carolers entered the house through one door, went up to the ballroom, and then went down and out the other side. Cissie poured the eggnog. This was an annual event until she was a teenager.

During her early teens the chauffeur/butler, Leroy Smith, taught Cissie how to drive.

When she and her younger brothers moved up to the third floor, they lobbied their mother to let them to claim one of the living rooms as a "hangout." She agreed. They had a Ping-Pong table and were allowed to paint the walls however they wished. A large mushroom painted over the fireplace mantel gave the room its name: the Mushroom. "The darkest hour is before dawn" was painted over the light switch. Cissie recounts that all her siblings went through the hippie stage, but there were no big parties, drinking, or drugs in the house.

Poltergeists?

The rocking chair in the McKissick bedroom rocked on its own. Doors shut, and lights went on and off on their own. Had President McKissick died in the McKissick room? Cissie remembers that the house staff wouldn't go in there alone—except once when Leroy Smith put ketchup on his white butler's jacket and lay down on the McKissick floor to scare his wife, Thelma, who also worked in the house.

Cissie reports that she saw a ghostly figure on the sun porch, a tall man wearing a black frock coat and a top hat.

One evening her parents were entertaining a couple, the husband of whom was being interviewed for a position. They brought along two children of similar age to Cissie and her younger brother, so Mrs. Jones suggested they all go up to the third floor and play Ping-Pong in the Mushroom. The children took the elevator (always fun), and they no sooner got into the first living room than suddenly the lights went out and the door closed shut. So Cissie's little brother, Andy, ran into the Mushroom, turned on all the lights, and opened the doors. The rest of the children followed him, as they were excited to play. Within minutes all the lights went out and the doors to the room slammed shut. All the children were so frightened that they ran down the back stairs to their parents.

After the guests were gone, President and Mrs. Jones were discussing how alarming that incident had been, a much more "direct" poltergeist experience than any previous one. And Cissie remembers her father concluding that the man was "dirty" and the ghosts were warning him of that. Warning heeded, the gentleman was not hired for the position.

A Fond Memory

Something that Cissie remembers as a highlight of her time in the President's House were the dinners where international students cooked a variety of ethnic foods that she had not previously been exposed to within her family.

On another note, the Jones children were quite industrious; they had a paper route in the neighborhood and would go to the candy warehouse, buy candy and drinks, and sell them to the students in front of the house on the Horseshoe. Cissie says they didn't make much money, but it was enough to keep them in candy.

Mary Alice and William Patterson at the retirement party for USC postmaster John Martin, with his wife, Catherine Pendleton Martin. Anna Durham, director of personnel, is pouring punch. UNIVERSITY ARCHIVES.

❧ 1974–1977: The Pattersons

The next residents of the President's House were twenty-fourth president William H. Patterson and his wife, Mary Alice Copeland Patterson.

The Pattersons were married later in life and had no children. I interviewed two of the Pattersons' friends to gain insight into their time on campus. Hal Brunton, who was vice president for business affairs, worked closely with President Patterson, and they were personal friends. In fact, prior to marrying Mary Alice Copeland, President Patterson brought dates to the Brunton home on Adger Road in Columbia.

Since he was responsible for the maintenance of university buildings, Mr. Brunton was familiar with the presidents' priorities with respect to the President's House. While Dr. Jones insisted that updates be confined to the public spaces in the house, President Patterson insisted the private quarters be renovated. Of course, after the Jones family, with five animal-loving children growing up in the house, the private quarters undoubtedly needed some attention during the Patterson administration.

Mr. Brunton contracted with Jack Scoville, a local designer to help with the facelift of the house. Mr. Brunton reports that, while Mrs. Jones delighted in the bubbles overflowing from her fountain after mischievous students added soap, those actions drove President and Mrs. Patterson crazy. One of their first endeavors was to move the fountain from the front of the house to the more protected back of the house.

Dick Webel of Innocenti and Webel, a well-known landscape-design firm in New York, was engaged to help beautify the rapidly growing campus. From the Russell administration, through the Jones and Patterson administrations, the campus grew from six thousand students to twenty-six thousand, and several new buildings were added to accommodate that growth. The GI Bill and the baby boom fed the surge in growth, and federal dollars were available to fund the building needs.

Mr. Brunton was concerned that the university would not be able to afford the services of Mr. Webel, a man whose reputation was on par with that of the likes of Frederick Law Olmsted, designer of Central Park. But as the fates would have it, Mr. Webel visited Spartanburg, South Carolina, four times a year to meet with Mr. Roger Milliken. A deal was struck that whenever Mr. Webel came to Spartanburg, he would make a side trip to the university to walk the property and share his guidance with Mr. Brunton, without the university incurring related travel expenses. On the days when Mr. Webel was in Columbia, Mr. Brunton set aside his other work and devoted 100 percent of his time to being with Mr. Webel.

Mr. Brunton asserted that Webel designed the patio area behind the President's House, the front of the Thomas Cooper Library, and the area around the Coliseum. He also gave direction on the plantings of the Horseshoe and the east side of campus, which from Capstone to Gambrell was all new. Mr. Brunton enjoyed sharing a tale of Webel's design for the the wide bridge over Pickens Street with planters on both sides, which created a virtual uprising among students pressuring the city to close Pickens to automobile traffic. The city scheduled a hearing during spring break, and the students were sure that was done intentionally to keep them away.

They came in droves and were vociferous in their charge. They failed because Pickens was one of the few major thoroughfares in the vicinity to run north to south, and the city could not restrict that access.

The Pattersons had many parties in the President's House. Since the executive leadership team consisted of only three members, the Bruntons were regularly there in receiving lines. Mrs. Brunton even remembers receiving guests once while on crutches.

Keith Davis, who was associate provost and research professor of psychology, was also friendly with the Pattersons. He remembers that "Pat" was a shy person. He preferred to socialize in small groups with people he knew well, and he and Mrs. Patterson didn't relate easily to the students. The Pattersons felt it was important to maintain a professional distance in order to control students. When I suggested that seemed unusual since he had been a professor, Mr. Davis said yes, but President Patterson had also been provost and secretary to the Board of Trustees, and Patterson thought it was important that the people running the university maintain order and promote respect for authority and traditions. It seems that Mrs. Patterson, whom Davis saw as a "Southern Belle," was of the same mind. He suggests that she abdicated some of her role to her special events coordinator to facilitate the social engagements.

Whether or not the Pattersons were the most comfortable hosts, the tradition of entertaining was carried on. President and Mrs. Patterson held pregame parties at the President's House prior to all football games. And a large annual all-faculty party was memorable.

Given their discomfort with entertaining large groups and attempts to keep a professional distance between the presidency and the rest of the community, it seems unusual that the Pattersons allowed guests to wander throughout the President's House, even in their private quarters. I am thankful that the practice of touring the family areas of the house and/or allowing guests to "wander" did not occur during the Palms and Sorensen administrations, so we did not inherit that precedent.

❧ 1977–1990: The Holderman Family

The next residents of the President's House were twenty-fifth president James B. Holderman, his wife, Carolyn Meadors Holderman, and their three daughters, Elizabeth (Betsy), Nancy, and Jamie.

The Holderman daughters have many memories of living here and were kind enough to share them with me.

Mrs. Holderman did her best to make the President's House a regular home for her daughters. The children lived in the kitchen as the center of activity and did their school work amidst the catering staff and partygoers. They had a window to a world of interesting guests; some even helped them with their homework. The kitchen was filled with the children's artwork, and their bedrooms looked like any other child's or teen's. During President Holderman's tenure, tours of the entire house were given, including the family quarters. Betsy described one occasion when she was home from high school, sick in bed, and heard a tour group coming through. She quickly made the bed and hid underneath it until the group passed!

When I mentioned writing this book to Betsy, the first story she told was about Missy, the Holderman's fourteen-year-old schnauzer, which passed away on a very cold day, half an hour before Mrs. Elizabeth Dole was due to arrive at the President's House for a visit. Mrs. Holderman knew that the ground was too frozen for a quick burial, so she wrapped Missy in a blue-striped towel and placed her in the freezer of the garden house to await a proper burial. Missy had many wonderful and not-so-wonderful experiences at the house. Groundskeepers captured her several times while attempting to catch cats and rodents. On occasion she ate rat poison, but she was a fighter and survived those episodes. She once warned the family of a burglar who entered the house and stole jewelry and a VCR. She relished all the festivities at the house and enjoyed the activity of the Horseshoe. She loved to tour the campus on her own and was frequently brought home by students. She lived a long life, and ultimately she was properly put to rest in the President's House garden.

Like the Jones children, the Holderman girls are convinced a ghost resides in the house on the third floor. The one they experienced was kind and loved to rock in an old rocking chair. The rocking chair was creaky and made quite a noise. The USC police responded once at three A.M. to check on an intruder who must have been the ghost. As Nancy led them around the room where she'd heard the noise, they had their guns drawn. Jamie was certain the ghost rode the elevator, so she left its inner gate open at night to prevent the ghost from using it as a vehicle to haunt or taunt. The spirit of Dr. J. Rion McKissick was evident through his eyes in the portrait that hung in the McKissick bedroom. According to the Holdermans, his eyes followed you everywhere you walked. (Could these have been the same eyes that followed Cissie Jones?)

The Holdermans enjoyed many guests at the President's House. These included foreign dignitaries, U.S. Supreme Court justices, athletes, actors, and former presidents Ford, Reagan, and George H. W. Bush. Jimmy Stewart played the piano and sang several songs for other guests. Dr. Henry Kissinger was particularly wonderful, coming into the kitchen to thank the kitchen staff. During President Ford's visit, the three girls went to McDonald's to get dinner, and the Secret Service would not allow them back into the house until they could prove their identity.

Some guests even answered the phone when it rang. It wasn't unusual for the Holderman girls to call home and have the phone answered by the likes of Helen Hayes.

On September 11, 1987, Pope John Paul II visited. It was a special and exciting day. That was the day Kevin Hall asked Jamie Holderman to marry him, and the Pope blessed them.

On another occasion, the Egyptian ambassador to the United States was visiting and praying upstairs in his room. Mrs. Holderman interrupted him thinking he was doing his "exercises." When he asked her which direction was east, she told him the wrong way and then had to interrupt him again when she realized her error. He told her not to worry, that Allah could probably hear his prayers from any direction.

After the long trip to South Carolina, the archbishop of Canterbury's wife wanted to iron his vestments—so Mrs. Holderman took her down to the laundry room, kept her company, and was regaled with stories of life in England.

With the Holdermans in residence, the ballroom (reception room) on the second floor was host to many events not related to ballroom dancing. The girls roller skated, hosted parties, and painted banners for football games there. Nancy even taught an aerobics class attended by Governor Carroll Campbell's wife and others.

Mrs. Jones's fountain was a favorite of the Holdermans. Jamie played with Barbies there, guests danced in the fountain, and the dog swam in it.

The Holderman daughters remember many parties at the

President and Mrs. Holderman with their daughters—Nancy and Betsy (standing) and Jamie (seated)—in the garden of the President's House. UNIVERSITY ARCHIVES.

house including law school, senior, and debutante festivities in the garden. On several occasions they filled the back patio with sand and hosted beach parties.

As for student activity on campus, the students made a habit of stealing the flags and Mrs. Holderman's decorations from the front of the house, but she was never angry. She just kept replacing them. Many students dropped by for information, directions, or just a good conversation. In those days the President's House was the center of protests, and on several occasions they went on all night. One particular time students put cement blocks in front of the front doors. Then there was the "Keep Coach McGuire Rally." Protestors put bumper stickers all over the front door of the President's House and on the family cars. The students demonstrated until late into the night.

Every once in a while a student would enjoy an evening too much and be found in the bushes or on the doorstep. His fellow mates pranked one poor student by placing him, his mattress, and a blanket in the President's House parking area. The next morning he was awakened, completely naked, by the USC police.

As it does today, snow on the Horseshoe brought out joyful play. When it snowed, students threw snowballs at each other or built snowmen on the front stoop.

The "Holderman girls" remember that the holidays were always fun with lots of people and unexpected guests. When they were eating at the dining-room table people would peer in through the floor-to-ceiling windows or drop by to ask a question. Mrs. Holderman frequently invited students with no families in town for a holiday meal. A highlight for the girls was when Heisman Trophy winner George Rogers, who loved Mrs. Holderman, came for dinner.

Interest in panty raids was still lingering in the 1970s, but Jamie remembers that when some students tried to get a panty raid going, President Holderman came out to let them know that there would be no interest in his daughters' unmentionables! As Mrs. Holderman was fond of saying, it all comes with "living above the store."

Mrs. Norma Palms and President John Palms in the library of the President's House. UNIVERSITY ARCHIVES.

❧ 1991–2002: The Palms Family

President John M. Palms and his wife, Norma Cannon Palms, were the next to make their home in the President's House. (President Palms followed Arthur Smith, who was interim president in 1990–1991. He and his wife, June, did not reside in the President's House but carried on the tradition of entertaining there.)

When Harris was being recruited to the position of dean of the School of Public Health, a dinner was held at the Faculty House (now known as McCutchen House). The hosts were President and Mrs. Palms and Provost and Mrs. Jerry Odom. I enjoyed meeting Toni Odom, a pharmacist who was also quite an athlete and a new mother, having recently adopted Ben. It is always easy to converse with someone who has a new baby because they are usually beaming and delight in everything their new little one does. Toni was no exception, and I still feel her joy after all these years. To this day I have a special bond with Toni and Jerry since Harris and I came to South Carolina coincidentally with Ben. I always know his age as I know the year was 1998.

Mrs. Palms was lovely and hospitable. She asked lots of sincere questions about our children, offering ideas for schools and activities that might interest them. After talking so much about our family, and not being aware of what the life of a First Lady at the University of South Carolina was like, I asked, "What do you like to do, Norma?" She didn't skip a beat: "To be perfectly honest with you, Patricia, I don't remember!" I've thought of her words many times since August 2008.

Mrs. Palms was the quintessential First Lady. She was warm and welcoming. It was important to her that guests felt at home in the President's House because she wanted everyone to leave "feeling that this is a university that really cares, a university that is excellent in every way, in hospitality, in academics, in sports and in people here."

Mrs. Palms remembers many notable individuals who visited the President's House during Dr. Palms's tenure as president. Hans-Dietrich Genscher was an early commencement speaker. As Mrs. Palms said, "He had just been involved in the reunification of Germany and that was a very interesting and historic time."

Archbishop Desmond Tutu gave the graduation address in December 1992 and stayed in the house. Dr. and Mrs. Palms had met him earlier when they were at Emory University. David McCullough, Pulitzer Prize–winning author

President and Mrs. Palms with Lady Carolina. UNIVERSITY ARCHIVES.

of *Truman,* and his wife, Rosalee, visited. Mrs. Palms recalls that "they were a really delightful couple. They said they wished they were southerners!"

Several journalists—including Bill Moyers, George Will, and Jim Hoagland—were guests at the President's House as well. When Mr. and Mrs. Hoagland stayed in the house, Mrs. Palms had a puppy named Lady Carolina. While everyone was enjoying the dinner for the honorary-degree recipient, Lady Carolina found her way to a delectable pair of shoes in the Kennedy bedroom and proceeded to chew one shoe from the pair Mrs. Hoagland was planning to wear to commencement the following day. Mrs. Hoagland was very gracious, writing that she had enjoyed a wonderful experience, but wasn't sure what to do with the other "doggone" shoe!

Mrs. Palms hosted many campus events annually. Some highlights were a student-athlete luncheon, receptions for Honors College freshmen and Phi Beta Kappa members and nominees, and a garden party for alumni celebrating their fiftieth college reunion.

She held an annual spirited Oktoberfest for all faculty, which featured German food, music, and, to my delight, dancing. I can say from having been her guest on many occasions that Mrs. Palms approached party planning with a whimsical spirit that encouraged participation. There were often songbooks for sing-alongs.

Once we were all asked to dress in clothing reminiscent of our high-school days. Fortunately I had kept several "period pieces" from my high-school years, so I wore a bright red crepe ensemble of wide bell-bottom pants and a shirred peasant top, circa 1970.

"Hospitality is an opening of one's self, one's heart, and one's soul to visitors," says Mrs. Palms. When asked how she balanced entertaining thousands of visitors with the loss of privacy, she concluded, "Where else can you have the chapel on the side, the library across from you, and a museum and a faculty house, and students coming and going to school and neighbors walking with children and grandchildren all around? It was an awesome experience."

Rose garden dedicated to Mrs. Palms in 2002. PHOTOGRAPH BY KEITH MCGRAW.

Mrs. Donna Sorensen and President Andrew Sorensen in the library of the President's House. PHOTOGRAPH BY PHIL SAWYER.

❧ 2002–2008: The Sorensen Family

Twenty-seventh president Andrew A. Sorensen and his wife, Donna Ingemie Sorensen, lived off campus initally, moving into the President's House after completion of extensive renovations.

I met Donna Sorensen back in 1983, when Dr. Andrew Sorensen arrived at the University of Massachusetts as dean of Public Health. Donna graciously hosted our family, toddler in tow, for Sunday dinner many times. Harris was up for tenure under the new dean, and it was a bit nerve racking, since Andrew's goal was to "raise the bar" on granting tenure. Fortunately Harris met the new expectations.

Years later, when Harris was dean of the Arnold School of Public Health, he invited Andrew to speak at its twenty-fifth anniversary. That was Andrew and Donna's first trip to the University of South Carolina, shortly after which he was nominated for the presidency. At Andrew's investiture dinner, Donna placed us with her extended family from the Boston area. We New Englanders ended up having the liveliest table in the place.

Another wonderful gift that Donna gave me was her philosophy on being a parent of adult children. As we had known one another's families from a young age, we would often share news of our children. We both understood the difficulty of wanting to guide our children but not intrude on their lives. Donna once told me something that I have since passed on to many other mothers: "A mother is only as happy as her least happy child." It remains reassuring even today to know that as mothers we share this universal experience and somehow find ways to support one another.

On a lighter note, during one Christmas season, Donna and I had met at multiple events. After about the fifth, I said to her, "Good evening, Donna, I hope you are well this evening. I have absolutely nothing new to report!" Donna shared some fond memories with me:

> Andrew and I had the privilege of decorating the newly renovated President's House. For eighteen months we lived off campus while the work on the house progressed. During that time I visited the house weekly and, with the assistance of Jane Evans, my special events director and talented interior decorator, was able to put the finishing touches on this historic home.
>
> The pleasure of living in this home was enhanced by the dedication of the people who worked in and around the house. We became a family, each day dealing with a new challenge and often celebrating a job well done, a birthday, a promotion, a birth, and comforting each other during an illness or death.

The serendipity of living on the Horseshoe was unparalleled. Andrew and I had an open-door policy, which was soon embraced by our students, especially our Horseshoe neighbors. One evening the doorbell rang unexpectedly. I went down to answer it, and there stood three students with a measuring cup. They were making sweet tea and wanted to borrow a cup of sugar. We were delighted to be asked and gave them the sugar. Two years later, as a member of the trio walked across the stage to shake Andrew's hand at Commencement, she handed him a bag of sugar and thanked him for the loan.

On another occasion, again in the evening, the doorbell rang, and there stood a student with six boxes of pizza. He was on his way to a party and thought we just might like to have a pizza for dinner.

The coup de grace came when we received a formal invitation to dinner from two seniors who lived in Harper College. We accepted and that evening walked across the Horseshoe to their room and, in that Lilliputian setting, experienced one of the most wonderful evenings of our entire tenure at USC. We were treated to insightful conversation and a beautiful meal (hors d'oeuvres to

President Sorensen presenting Mrs. Sorensen's birthday surprise. PHOTOGRAPH BY PHIL SAWYER.

The lower garden, suggested by Mrs. Sorensen to replace a parking area with expanded entertaining space. PHOTOGRAPH BY KEITH MCGRAW.

dessert) all prepared from scratch by these students.

Andrew opened the President's House to all. The community and the university became partners in growth and development, and that process began by breaking bread together. The President's House was the perfect setting for many joyful and productive dinners.

National figures also graced our home. President George W. Bush, presidential candidate Barack Obama and Michelle Obama, vice-presidential candidate Joe Biden, and Supreme Court Chief Justice John Roberts all spent time in the formal living room with us, greeting the university and Columbia communities.

We especially enjoyed having faculty, staff, and students celebrate the holidays with us as well as precommencement celebrations. The President's House is truly a home to the entire university community.

There were certainly many memorable personal moments. Our nine-month grandson, Art, meeting Cocky for the first time and being both fascinated and shy; our son Aaron, walking with an older, jet-lagged Art to

IHOP at 3 A.M. because Art was so excited to be in the U.S. and couldn't sleep; and especially all the games of pick-up soccer he and Art played on the Horseshoe.

Our son Ben recalls playing football on the Horseshoe with family and students during Thanksgiving vacations; the second-floor kitchen being remodeled, and Andrew making avocado and cheese sandwiches for lunch; but especially he recalls the incredibly gracious staff that made us feel truly at home.

If I may add one of my memories of the Sorensens' tenure in the President's House to Donna's, it would be the love that beamed through Andrew's eyes as he donned a chef's hat and delivered an Italian cream cake to Donna on her birthday every year during the August honorary-degree-recipient dinner.

This beautiful cake was baked by Rick Gant, former USC Sodexo catering manager and currently general manager of Coker College Dining Services, Sodexo On-Site Solutions. His recipe, which is included in part 3, is deliciously decadent, moist, nutty, and sweet. I would definitely recommend it!

Major Renovations to the President's House

The greatest change to the house itself came in the 1950s, when the Russells decided to confront the poor condition of the nearly one-hundred-year-old McKissick-Wauchope House and convert it to a single family dwelling for the university president's residence. They did the university a great favor. They glorified the building with broad functional changes such as removing walls and adding porches. They also brought wonderful architectural features, such as beautiful brass hardware, Virginia-pine mantelpieces, and the precious 1811 French wallpaper that graces the reception room. Depicting a Chinese wedding procession, it encompasses more than forty-six feet of nonrepeating detail. The most fascinating part to me is that it was made by block printing.

Detail of the 1811 French wall covering in the President's House reception room. PHOTOGRAPH BY KEITH MCGRAW.

The carved pine mantelpiece in the President's House library. PHOTOGRAPH BY KEITH MCGRAW.

The newly expanded gardens of the President's House, circa 2004. UNIVERSITY ARCHIVES.

The current President's House is a magnificent showplace that has two functions. It provides an elegant event space for the University of South Carolina community and guests, and a home for the president and his (I'm sure one day "her") family.

By 1974 renovations were needed in the private quarters of the house. In particular the back porches on the second and third floors were enclosed to create sunrooms that could be used year round.

In 2002 the Board of Trustees decided to conduct some major mechanical and structural updates. A new roof was installed, and windows were repaired. Updated plumbing was required, and all eight bathrooms were redone. Electrical wiring was updated, and new alarm systems were installed. Old fan-coil heating and air units were replaced with modern central heating and air-conditioning. And, to my delight, a kitchen was added on the second floor, within what we commonly call "our apartment." Mrs. Palms has recounted that, during her time as First Lady, she had to dress before going downstairs for her morning coffee.

The garden was also updated during this renovation. A parking lot on the west side closest to Legare was replaced by a large brick patio and enclosed within a brick wall to become part of the backyard. On the east side of the garden, closest to Rutledge, a work area for lawn and garden equipment was contracted by about two-thirds to enhance the entertainment area. Since this renovation, the President's House garden has had three distinct sections—the upper, middle, and lower gardens—which together have accommodated up to approximately six hundred guests, serving us well on many occasions.

In 2009 an organic vegetable garden was planted on the west side of the President's House garden at the entrance to the parking enclosure. Formerly the site of an ailing oak tree, this area was given new life and purpose as a vegetable garden after the tree was removed. Discussions with the director of Sustainable Carolina and a committee of students interested in issues of sustainability on campus inspired the addition of rain barrels to the gutter at a back corner of the house so the water could be used for irrigating the garden. They also

The President's House vegetable garden. PHOTOGRAPH BY KEITH MCGRAW.

Raised beds cultivated by students, faculty, and staff at USC. PHOTOGRAPH BY KEITH MCGRAW.

The 2014 greenhouse connected to the President's House garden. PHOTOGRAPH BY KEITH MCGRAW.

inspired the President's House compost, used to make organic fertilizer from kitchen and garden waste. Vegetables from the garden are served at events in the house and are often distributed at the Healthy Carolina Farmers Market.

Interest in vegetable gardening prompted Outdoor Recreation, a club on campus, to apply for a grant to construct raised beds that could be cultivated by students, faculty, and staff. As a result of their efforts, we now have twenty raised beds on the east end of Preston Green adjacent to the President's House organic vegetable garden. The location allows us to share water and compost material, as well as seedlings started in the new greenhouse.

The renovation of the old Arnold School of Public Health building on the corner of Greene and Sumter Streets for the School of Journalism and Mass Communication, College of Information and Communications, required the razing of an old greenhouse, which stood on the Sumter Street side of the building, behind the brick wall that encircles the Horseshoe.

At the time of its demise, the greenhouse was used by the President's House horticulturist to house ferns and potted palms used campus-wide for events, to revive orchids that had faded for reuse in dish gardens for presidential events, to start seedlings for botanicals and garden fruits and vegetables used at the President's House on the Horseshoe and around Russell House, to store off-season potted garden plants and to create and store container gardens used for presidential events. Though the old greenhouse was in disrepair and was located on land that was needed by the College of Information and Communications, it was quite a loss to the horticulture team serving the President's House, the Horseshoe, and Russell House.

As a result, the Board of Trustees approved construction of a smaller, more decorative greenhouse that would connect to the President's House garden. In the fall of 2014 the President's House greenhouse, a Victorian-style conservatory painted Charleston green, was completed. In addition to

Mrs. Jones's fountain as seen through the window in the President's House foyer. PHOTOGRAPH BY KEITH MCGRAW.

One of our pomegranates. PHOTOGRAPH BY KEITH MCGRAW.

satisfying horticultural needs, the new greenhouse has become an educational showcase for interesting plants, especially heirloom varieties.

The President's House welcomes thirty-five hundred guests annually, so it gets quite a bit of traffic. Wear and tear is attended to regularly, but at certain times sheer age and food and drink mishaps take their toll, and more extensive work is required. During the summer of 2014, the first floor of the house was given a facelift. Rugs were removed for cleaning and mending, and furniture was repaired, reupholstered, or replaced. Wallpaper was replaced in the two dining rooms, and new draperies were made for the front dining room. The back dining room inherited the draperies that had hung in the front room. One extra pair of draperies from the front room now adorns the window in the foyer, a bonus as it frames the fountain beautifully.

During the winter of 2015 a project was initiated to reroute rainwater that had been flooding the lower-level laundry room of the house and to improve the lighting in the garden for safety and security. The project required weeks of deep hand trenching throughout the garden beds. Those of us who cherish the garden held our breath fearing damage to our beloved plants. I was particularly concerned about a pomegranate tree that we had planted four years earlier. The first year it yielded one fruit, but the harvest has been steadily increasing. In fall 2014 it peaked at twenty-two pomegranates. We were thankful when the pomegranate budded again the following spring. The first major rainstorm left not a drop in the laundry room, and all areas of the garden are well lit to ensure the safety of our guests.

PART TWO

The House and First Family Today

A Tour of the House and Gardens

The dual front doors of the President's House are a reminder that the house was built as a duplex. The two doors are useful during receptions, as we use the main door on the Rutledge side as the entrance and the one on the Legare side as the egress. The doors also provide a backdrop for adding color and decoration to the front of the house. The horticulturist often arranges green and flowering plants in large moss-lined wrought-iron baskets. The photographs included here present a sample of seasonal decorations.

The stately President's House at the University of South Carolina, 2016. PHOTOGRAPH BY KEITH MCGRAW.

Seasonal door decorations. PHOTOGRAPHS BY KEITH MCGRAW.

The east foyer. PHOTOGRAPH BY KEITH MCGRAW.

❧ The Main Entrance

We generally welcome our guests in the east foyer of the house. They've usually received name tags outside on the Horseshoe from Presidential Student Ambassadors, wonderful representatives of our student body who also help with logistics. This group is a subset of about twelve of the approximately one hundred Student Ambassadors who lead tours for the USC Welcome Center.

In the foyer there are three noteworthy pieces. The first, *View of Charleston from Mt. Pleasant,* is a pastel by Elizabeth O'Neill Verner. Dr. Verner, who was a native of Charleston, was awarded the honorary degree of Doctor of Literature by the University in 1947. As an artist of the Charleston Renaissance in the 1920s and 1930s, she created realistic land- and cityscapes in pastels and etching. She developed a process that became known as "Verner Colors," drawing with pastels

on raw silk while it was still wet from the glue used to hold it to a board. This process created longer-lasting color. In addition to lowcountry scenes, she also painted some of the historic buildings on the Horseshoe.

The second is *A New Description of Carolina,* a 1676 map by John Speed. It was heavily based on the exploration of John Lederer and on Ogilby's Lords Proprietors' map of 1674. This seminal map represents one of the earliest attempts to chart the Carolina interior. Oriented to the west, it covers an area from the Spanish colony of St. Augustine, Florida, north to Jamestown, Virginia, and extends inland as far as the Appalachian (Apalathean) Mountains.

The third piece of interest sits on a large writing desk toward the back of the foyer. It's a French gilt bronze and marble double inkwell with a central gamecock figure. The late-nineteenth-century inkwell was donated by Caroline McKissick Dial.

View of Charleston from Mt. Pleasant, by Elizabeth O'Neill Verner, 1964. Donated by Mrs. Ora Lee Dantzler in 2005 in memory of her husband, Marion Dantzler. USC McKissick Museum Collection.

PHOTOGRAPH BY KEITH MCGRAW.

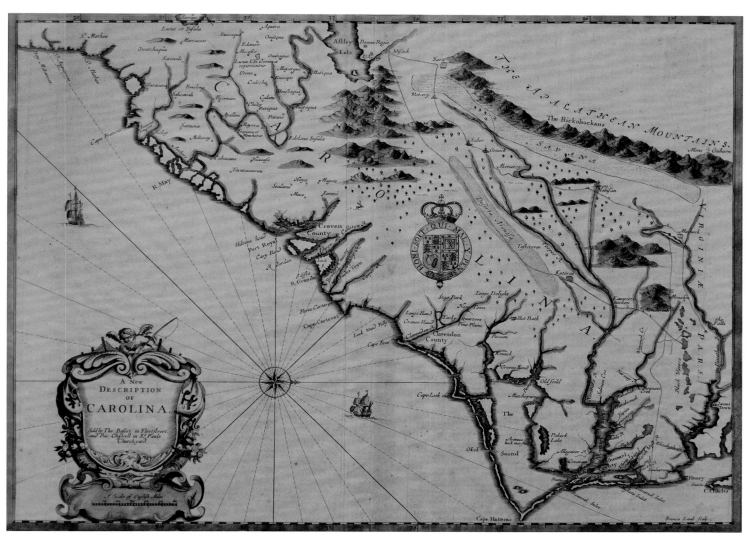

A New Description of Carolina, 1676, map by John Speed. Engraved by Francis Lamb.
South Caroliniana Library Collection. PHOTOGRAPH BY KEITH MCGRAW.

Late-nineteenth-century gamecock inkwell donated by Caroline McKissick Dial.
PHOTOGRAPH BY KEITH MCGRAW.

A view of the library facing the garden. PHOTOGRAPHS BY KEITH MCGRAW.

❧ The Library

The library is a 718-square-foot room, which has floor-to-ceiling windows of blown-glass panes overlooking the Horseshoe and two large windows with a view of the patio behind the house. The western wall has two fireplaces and is covered with built-in bookcases; the eastern wall is raised panels. On the eastern wall in the center of the room hangs *Marion and His Men in the Swamp,* an oil on canvas painted by William D. Washington in about 1865. The painting depicts Marion and his men around a campfire. Early in his career, the artist worked at the U.S. Patent Office in Washington, D.C., and he studied in Germany with Emanuel Leutze. Washington was a founder of the Washington Art Association and taught for a time at Virginia Military Institute. The painting was purchased by a private individual at a sale of the Rosenthal Collection and donated to USC.

Marion and His Men in the Swamp, circa 1865, by William D. Washington. Oil on canvas.
South Caroliniana Library Collection. PHOTOGRAPH BY KEITH MCGRAW.

Overleaf: View of the library facing the historic Horseshoe. PHOTOGRAPH BY KEITH MCGRAW.

Another view of the library. PHOTOGRAPH BY KEITH MCGRAW.

Also in the library is a large oval, oriental, pierced and carved hardwood and marble table, circa 1860. The table has three distinct tiers of elaborate carving.

A noble George III mahogany tall case clock brings the library to life on the hour. Distinguished by a broken arch, dentil molding, and blind fretwork crown-over-column supports, it rests on shaped bracket feet.

Oriental hardwood and marble table, circa 1860. PHOTOGRAPH BY KEITH MCGRAW.

George III mahogany tall case clock, circa 1810. Donated by Evelyn L. Kendall and family in 1960. PHOTOGRAPH BY KEITH MCGRAW.

The front dining room with its 1930s Czechoslovakian crystal chandelier. PHOTOGRAPH BY KEITH MCGRAW.

◈ The Front Dining Room

The front dining room is an elegant space, with a fireplace and nine-foot-tall blown-glass pane windows looking onto the world of the Horseshoe. It has a double-pedestal, Sheraton-style mahogany table with mahogany Chippendale-style chairs that can accommodate up to twelve guests. The sideboard is mahogany in the Hepplewhite Sheraton style. There are two half-moon tables against the west wall of the room. Various silver pieces are displayed in the front dining room. One has an interesting provenance. It's a Victorian silver-plated soup tureen with an acorn finial (a most appropriate decoration for the Horseshoe). Made by the Ames Manufacturing Company of Chicopee, Massachusetts, the Sheffield-style tureen, circa 1850, is oval and lightly chased. The lip of the tureen has a raised, beaded design; the legs and handles are attached with a raised leaf and acorn design. The piece belonged to George and Sarah Wolfe Heyman. He was a prosperous wood and coal merchant in Chester, South Carolina. It was donated to USC in 1982 by Margaret M. Heyman, Ph. D.

Silver-plated soup tureen, circa 1850. USC McKissick Museum Collection. PHOTOGRAPH BY KEITH MCGRAW.

When General Sherman's troops were on their march to the sea, the Heyman family wrapped the tureen and other family silver in burlap and hid them in the well behind their house. This special piece was "well preserved."

A lovely Czechoslovakian crystal chandelier that dates to the 1930s provides the central lighting in the front dining room. With its old cross-and-cut design it elevates the elegance of the room.

The back dining room with its 1920s Czechoslovakian crystal chandelier. PHOTOGRAPH BY KEITH MCGRAW.

❧ The Back Dining Room

Another, equally elegant, Czechoslovakian crystal chandelier, which dates from the early 1920s, hangs in the back dining room.

The back dining room has a beautiful square mahogany table. A silver cabinet houses engraved pieces from the collections of several prominent South Carolinians. The grouping includes cups, plates, pitchers, platters, covered dishes, and a delicate "bride's basket" decorated with wheat and grapes.

There are two companion paintings by William Harrison Scarborough on the fireplace wall in the back dining room. Painted around 1850, they depict views of the university campus shortly after the construction of the South Caroliniana Library. Scarborough moved to Columbia around 1843 and established a three-room studio facing Marion Street. Spending thirty years of his forty-year career in Columbia, he painted primarily in oils and specialized in portraits. His subjects included governors, military figures, and prominent members of USC and Columbia society. Among them were Dr. Joseph LeConte, Francis Lieber, William Preston, and Colonel Wade Hampton. Originally in the collection of Henry Buist, an 1847 graduate of South Carolina College, the paintings were purchased by the South Caroliniana Library from Herman Schindler of Charleston in 1952.

North and South Sides of the Horseshoe, circa 1850, by William Harrison Scarborough.
South Caroliniana Library Collection. PHOTOGRAPHS BY KEITH MCGRAW.

The West Foyer and Second-Floor Landings

In the west foyer of the house lies an antique Persian Lilihan rug, which dates to approximately 1900 and comes from the estate of James F. Byrnes. The Sarouk Village pattern is a large, symmetrical floral design—with rich rose and navy colors. Also in the west foyer is an American Sheraton sofa believed to date to around 1820. It is also from the Byrnes estate and is presumed to have belonged to Mrs. Byrnes's mother.

Hanging on the wall above the sofa are two watercolors, the work of etymologist and ornithologist John Abbot (1751–1840), a near contemporary of Audubon, Laurens, and Bartram. These works were part of a collection of more than fifteen thousand natural-history watercolors, woodcuts, engravings, lithographs, and maps given to the university by W. Graham Arader in 2011. The Arader Collection is intended for use as a dynamic teaching tool, and pieces hang in classrooms, hallways, offices, and conference rooms in more than thirty buildings on campus. Selected for the President's House because they represent birds found in South Carolina, the *Indigo Bunting* and *Boat Tailed Grackle* watercolors (circa 1823) are exceptionally rare.

On the east landing between the first and second floors lies another rug from the Byrnes collection. This one is an antique Persian Sarouk, also dating to approximately 1900. Its design is smaller and more refined.

On the same landing is a chest that holds a pair of Chinese export armorial urns with covers. These graceful porcelains were brought to my attention by Ron Long of Charlton Hall, an auction gallery in Columbia, South Carolina. The

The American Sheraton sofa and Persian Lilihan rug in the west foyer. Estate of James F. Byrnes. PHOTOGRAPH BY KEITH MCGRAW.

Boat Tail Grackle and *Indigo Bunting,* watercolors by John Abbot, circa 1823. Gift of W. Graham Arader, 2011.

PHOTOGRAPHS BY KEITH MCGRAW.

Mahogany secretary, circa 1831. McKissick Museum Collection.

PHOTOGRAPH BY KEITH MCGRAW.

Two sides of a pair of armorial urns with covers, circa 1800. PHOTOGRAPH BY KEITH MCGRAW.

vessels are about sixteen inches tall with a white field and multicolor floral design. They appear to be authentic Chinese export armorial urns. Their coat of arms displays a red dragon atop a helmeted knight in armor. His shield, a blue and gold checkerboard, is banded by a red sash bearing a black crescent. Long's suspicion is that these are market pieces dating most probably from 1790 to 1820. The coat of arms for such pieces could be English or European.

On the west landing outside the reception room is a large mahogany secretary formerly owned by Mrs. Joseph Addison Black. Her father ordered it from Philadelphia in 1831 as a wedding gift for her. It was shipped from Charleston to Columbia on a cotton boat. Martha Black Wallace, the Blacks' granddaughter, donated it to the university in 1926. The large decorative drawer opens to create a drop-front secretary with fitted interiors.

Overleaf: Long view of the reception room with its circa 1811 Procession Chinoise wallcovering. PHOTOGRAPH BY KEITH MCGRAW.

❧ The Reception Room (Ballroom)

The 1811 French wallpaper, in the Procession Chinoise pattern, is an exceptionally rare block-printed wallcovering.

It was first introduced to me as Zuber paper, having been portrayed as such in a February 13, 1975, letter from the Metropolitan Museum of Art in response to a request from George Curry, secretary to the USC Board of Trustees. But when I began my research on the furnishings of the house, I suspected the wallpaper had been misidentified as Zuber's Le Décor Chinois. In a quick internet search I saw illustrations of Le Décor Chinois, which features natural scenes including flowers, trees, and bird life, but not an elaborate mural such as ours. Nor did I find anything like ours when I searched Zuber murals. I was then directed to two historic-wallpaper reference books but found neither to be definitive. Later, in the records of the President's House I read an assessment of the paper by T. K. McClintock Ltd, a firm in Somerville, Massachusetts, which was retained to conserve the paper in 1998. Here is that company's characterization of the paper in the record of the conservation:

> The wallpaper is a panoramic design depicting a Chinese procession, printed in France between 1811–1820, the designer and manufacturer of which are not recorded. The design was relief printed with wood blocks using opaque mineral pigments in a grisaille/sepia palette in a glue binder (tempura) onto 20 inch wide rolls made from joined sheets of handmade laid paper (measuring 16.5 by 20 inches). . . . A complete set of Procession Chinoise originally numbered 30 rolls, of which 28 full and partial rolls are mounted on the walls of the Reception Room. . . . . Three other sets of Procession Chinoise are recorded in European collections. (Nouvel-

Detail of the Procession Chinoise wallcovering. PHOTOGRAPH BY KEITH MCGRAW.

The circa 1790–1820 George III carved mahogany console table in the reception room. PHOTOGRAPH BY KEITH MCGRAW.

Detail of the coat of arms on the George III console table. PHOTOGRAPH BY KEITH MCGRAW.

65

Nineteenth-century oriental carved bench in the reception room. PHOTOGRAPH BY KEITH MCGRAW.

Kammerer, Odile. "Papiers Peints Panaramiques," Musée des Arts Décoratifs, Paris 1990, 308–9)

To be certain Lisa Robinette sent photographs of the paper to the New York office of Zuber, which sent them along to Paris for authentication. They concurred with T. K. McClintock that the paper is French in origin but not Zuber.

Since I frequently show our special wallpaper to our many guests, I am happy to have the correct information to share. And while I'm a touch sad to lose the Zuber connection as so many people are familiar with this prestigious company, our paper is actually older than I originally thought.

In addition to its beautiful wallcovering, the reception room is furnished with two elaborately carved George III mahogany console tables. Upon examination it appears one table is period, possibly crafted in Ireland around 1790–1820, while the second is a reproduction made later to create a pair. A coat of arms is carved above the center leg of each table.

An oriental nineteenth-century carved mahogany bench sits under the reception-room windows overlooking the Horseshoe. The back of the bench has three carved panels. The two outer panels are of branches and birds, and the central panel depicts two horses.

Detail of the central panel of the nineteenth-century bench. PHOTOGRAPH BY KEITH MCGRAW.

One of the reception room chandeliers. PHOTOGRAPH BY KEITH MCGRAW.

The historic ecumenical meeting during Pope John Paul II's visit to USC in 1987. PHOTOGRAPH BY KEITH MCGRAW.

The two large crystal chandeliers in the reception room are a perfect size for the 735-square-foot room. Mr. and Mrs. Walter Keenan donated the chandeliers in the 1980s to replace smaller crystal chandeliers, which the Keenans identified as being the wrong scale for the room. They found a beautiful, much larger chandelier and had a second one made as its companion. The original smaller chandeliers now hang in the halls at either end of the reception room, creating an elegant entry and egress from this palatial space.

On September 27, 1987, His Holiness Pope John Paul II addressed thousands of University of South Carolina students on the historic Horseshoe. A plaque located beside the west portico reminds all of his words, which brought cheers from the students:

It is wonderful to be young,
It is wonderful to be young and to be a student,
It is wonderful to be young and to be a student at the University of South Carolina.

As one of many security measures that were taken in advance of the Pope's visit, all the students who resided in the dormitories on the Horseshoe had to be relocated for twenty-four hours prior to his visit. I am told they had T-shirts made up that said, "I was moved by the Pope!"

During his visit, Pope John Paul II also presided over a historic ecumenical meeting of twenty-seven denominational leaders in the reception room of the President's House and rested in the John F. Kennedy bedroom.

❧ East Landing outside Reception Room

An antique chair adapted and upholstered by Joseph S. Czartosieski, of Peconic, New York, especially for Pope John Paul II's visit now sits on the east landing just outside the reception room. This chair has become more significant over time. With the canonization of Pope John Paul II, Karol Józef Wojtyla, to sainthood on April 27, 2014, the chair became a "relic of the second class," or an "authentic contact relic," an object touched by a saint in his or her lifetime.

Hanging above Pope Saint John Paul's chair is a Margaret Carter print symbolizing the ecumenical year at the university. Depicted with Pope John Paul II are the Reverend Billy Graham, Christian evangelist; Archbishop Iakovos, primate of the Greek Orthodox Archdiocese of North and South America; and the Most Reverend Robert Runcie, archbishop of Canterbury.

In the same hall stands an impressive ten-foot-tall Victorian pier mirror. Most mirrors in this style originated in New York and were made from carved wood, gesso, and gilt. This one has curved scrolling and a pierced floral-and-fruit-work pediment with a rope-twist-designed frame. The base is raised on cabriole legs and topped with white marble. It dates to approximately 1860.

Eagle carving on chair, which Czartosieski selected in part because the eagle is a national symbol of Saint Pope John Paul II's native Poland. PHOTOGRAPH BY KEITH MCGRAW.

The Pope Saint John Paul II chair and the Margaret Carter commemorative print. PHOTOGRAPH BY KEITH MCGRAW.

Victorian pier mirror on the east landing. PHOTOGRAPH BY KEITH MCGRAW.

❧ The President's Family Quarters

Behind the reception room is the president's private quarters, affectionately known as "the apartment." The bedrooms in the apartment were furnished when we moved in, and we supplied living room and kitchen furnishings. Here we have our art collection, library, and family photographs. This is the place in the house where we retreat at the close of the day, whenever the last event ends. It has a living room, two bedrooms, a kitchen, and a sun porch. I use the second bedroom as an office, but I have not removed the twin beds, for when family comes from out of town, we need all the beds the house has to offer and then some.

In recent years one section of the enclosed sun porch has gradually been converted to a playroom for our grandchildren. One might question why, given that they live in California and don't get to South Carolina very often. The answer is simple. I wanted the first sentence from our granddaughter Penelope's mouth to be, "I want to go to Mimi's house!" So I set out to make Mimi's house, at least the part she would become most familiar with, every child's dream. It has a retro kitchen, with appliances and wooden foods, books, puzzles, and dolls. And she knows it well, as does little sister, Alice, because this is the place I "FaceTime" from! Sometimes we do a puzzle together, and other times we make a stew. I count on the girls to tell me what ingredients to use and in what quantities, and I follow their directions. Penelope tells me which toppings to Velcro to her wooden pizza, and what temperature to set the oven. Alice has had a favorite toy—the singing teakettle—since before she could speak. It has always prompted her to dance.

Playroom for the Pastides grandchildren. PHOTOGRAPH BY KEITH MCGRAW.

The den and kitchen in the family quarters. PHOTOGRAPH BY KEITH MCGRAW.

❧ The Third-Floor West Landing

On the west landing between the second and third floors is a Chinese carved hardwood chest. The top of the chest is arched, and the legs are slightly bowed. The entire chest is carved with scenes of figures on boats surrounded by landscape. This chest was a gift from Madame Chiang Kai-shek to James F. Byrnes.

Detail of the carving on the Chinese chest. PHOTOGRAPH BY KEITH MCGRAW.

Chinese carved hardwood chest, first half of the twentieth century. Estate of James F. Byrnes. PHOTOGRAPH BY KEITH MCGRAW.

The John F. Kennedy bedroom. PHOTOGRAPH BY KEITH MCGRAW.

❧ The John F. Kennedy Bedroom

At the top of the west staircase is the John F. Kennedy bedroom. Senator Kennedy was the University's commencement speaker on May 31, 1957, and the room overlooks the Horseshoe, where the commencement took place. Photographs in the room show Senator Kennedy with President Russell, Governor George B. Timmerman Jr., and the Honorable James F. Byrnes.

As the story goes, the national Democratic Party recommended Senator Kennedy as commencement speaker because they knew he would need to garner support from the southern states if he were to be a successful United States presidential candidate. His hailing from Massachusetts, having a different accent, and being Roman Catholic were all factors that had the potential to be negatives for southern voters. Call the party's motive testing the waters or trying to sell their candidate. In either case the university accepted, and Senator Kennedy traveled to South Carolina with a prepared speech.

The most interesting part of the story comes when the senator looked over his speech the night before commencement and edited it, making it the speech he wanted to deliver to our students. In the now "Kennedy bedroom," he reworked the original version, which was typed on onionskin paper. Kennedy drew comparisons between the histories

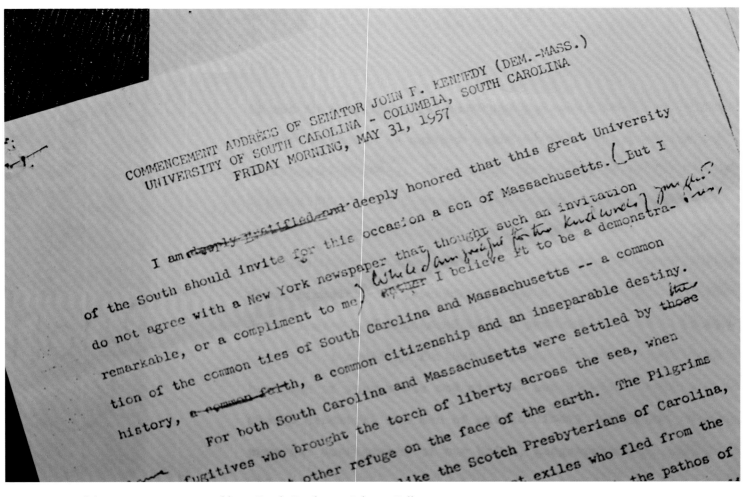

COMMENCEMENT ADDRESS OF SENATOR JOHN F. KENNEDY (DEM.-MASS.)
UNIVERSITY OF SOUTH CAROLINA - COLUMBIA, SOUTH CAROLINA
FRIDAY MORNING, MAY 31, 1957

I am deeply gratified and deeply honored that this great University of the South should invite for this occasion a son of Massachusetts. But I do not agree with a New York newspaper that thought such an invitation remarkable, or a compliment to me. While I am grateful for the kind words, I believe it to be a demonstration of the common ties of South Carolina and Massachusetts -- a common history, a common faith, a common citizenship and an inseparable destiny. For both South Carolina and Massachusetts were settled by those fugitives who brought the torch of liberty across the sea, when other refuge on the face of the earth. The Pilgrims like the Scotch Presbyterians of Carolina, exiles who fled from the pathos of

Senator Kennedy's 1957 commencement address. South Caroliniana Library Collection.
PHOTOGRAPH BY KEITH MCGRAW.

of the states of Massachusetts and South Carolina and the tenacity with which their early citizens, many fugitives, built states that sought to offer refuge from tyranny. He bemoaned the fact that politics and scholarship have drifted apart and encouraged our students to engage their learned minds with the political realm to solve the problems of our times. After giving the address, Senator Kennedy left it on the podium, and it is now part of the South Caroliniana Library collection.

The Kennedy bedroom is home to a lovely Queen Anne highboy, which dates to 1780. Made from American walnut, it sits on cabriole legs, has a decorative broken-arch-design top, and two beautifully carved shell-front drawers.

Facing page and above detail: Queen Anne highboy, circa 1780. Donated by Mrs. Evelyn L. Kendall and family, 1960. PHOTOGRAPHS BY KEITH MCGRAW.

❧ The J. Rion and Caroline McKissick Bedroom

The J. Rion and Caroline McKissick bedroom houses a collection of their furniture, including an American Sheraton four-poster canopy bed from 1800. The upper section of each turned post is fluted. The lower section has a leaf-shaped design. The carved headboard is scrolled. The crocheted valance has a gamecock design. The McKissick room is very sunny in the afternoon, so we try to protect the valance by partially closing the shutters. On the wall opposite the bed is an American mahogany secretary desk dating from approximately 1810. It has a Greek key design, and the glass front (probably added later) has thirteen panels of fretwork.

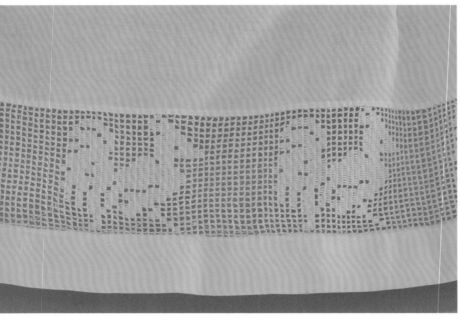

Detail of the crocheted valence on the American Sheraton bed.
PHOTOGRAPH BY KEITH MCGRAW.

The McKissick bedroom. McKissick Collection. PHOTOGRAPH BY KEITH MCGRAW.

❧ The Byrnes and Koger Bedrooms

There are two other large bedrooms on the third floor, named for the families who donated the furnishings. The Byrnes room is home to a set of Sheraton chairs with pegged construction and hand carving on the arms. These features suggest that the chairs may date to anywhere between 1740 and 1820. When the chairs require reupholstery, we will examine them more closely, but their pegged construction is evident. Each of the four bedrooms on the third floor has its own bathroom.

The Byrnes bedroom. PHOTOGRAPH BY KEITH MCGRAW.

The Koger bedroom. PHOTOGRAPH BY KEITH MCGRAW.

⚘ The Third-Floor East Landing and Hallway

On the third floor east landing there is a beautiful southern American walnut hunt board from 1790. It has a rectangular top over a configuration of short drawers and panel doors, resting on square tapered legs. This piece was made in South Carolina and was acquired from the estate of Mrs. Jennie Haddock Feagle.

The third-floor hallway has an antique Persian Hamadan rug, which dates from 1890. The runner has geometric patterns in multiple colors set on a brick background.

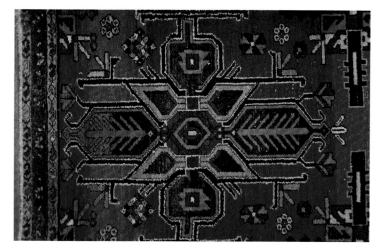

Detail of the Persian Hamadan rug in the third-floor hallway, circa 1890. PHOTOGRAPH BY KEITH MCGRAW.

Southern American walnut hunt board on the third-floor east landing, circa 1790. Estate of Mrs. Jennie Haddock Feagle. PHOTOGRAPH BY KEITH MCGRAW.

Above and following pages: Two views of the "man cave" with its Gamecock athletics collections.
PHOTOGRAPHS BY KEITH MCGRAW.

❧ The Third-Floor Living Room and Recreation Room

In the center of the third floor are two large rooms; one used as a living room for guests is equipped with a television and coffee service. It has many pieces of furniture from the Byrnes estate.

The other central room on the third floor is the "man cave." This room houses a pool table (thanks to the Sorensen sons, who urged their dad to purchase it) and an ever-growing collection of Gamecock sports memorabilia. There you can see a framed football jersey bearing the number 28, for Harris, the twenty-eighth president, along with a large framed photograph from the opening pitch thrown out at the new Gamecock baseball park. That is a story I love to tell because Carolina Stadium (now Founders Park) opened on

Harris's birthday in 2009. He was invited to throw out the first pitch alongside two former USC baseball coaches, June Raines and Bobby Richardson, formerly a star player with the New York Yankees. I've rarely seen Harris more excited about meeting someone than he was when he met Bobby Richardson for the first time. He later told me, "When I was a kid, I wanted to *be* Bobby Richardson!"

The room hosts lots of headlines about USC's back-to-back 2010 and 2011 College World Series wins, signed baseballs, and a crazy-happy parade photograph after the second championship. I will never forget that parade through downtown Columbia, when I called out to our fans, "Let's go for three!" Coach Tanner, who was riding in the car directly behind us, was a bit wary of my enthusiasm!

We also have a signed print of our *first ever* NCAA title in any sport, won by the 2002 women's track and field team,

whom we hosted during their tenth reunion on campus. Two members of that team have won Olympic medals. Aleen Bailey won a gold medal in the 4×100-meter relay at the 2004 Olympics in Athens. The other was Lashinda Demus, whose hurdling won her a silver medal in the 2012 London Olympics. We celebrated with her family when she completed her bachelor's degree online in 2015 through Palmetto College. Another national championship in 2015 was among the many titles earned by the USC equestrian team, led by Coach Boo Major. Harris and I cherish the rings we were given in honor of this victory. For a president few things compare to a collection of sixteen rings in five sports (so far)!

Football takes up much of the room, touting our three eleven-win seasons, three ESPN GameDays on the Horseshoe, and significant bowl victories. A picture signed by quarterback Connor Shaw commemorates the fifth-straight win against Clemson. Also included is a picture of "The Hit" autographed by Jadeveon Clowney. We hold a special place in our hearts for number 21, Marcus Lattimore. Among various mementos and photos is a beautiful letter Marcus wrote to us that we will always cherish. We have several special footballs, including one Coach Steve Spurrier sent to me for being a faithful fan and one signed by President George and Mrs. Barbara Bush inscribed, "Go Gamecocks!"

Women's basketball has given us so much to cheer about, and their memorabilia include record books, tee shirts, tournament passes, basketballs, and lots of photographs.

In 2017 we joyfully expanded the collection to include more tickets, hats, and tee shirts from the Final Four. We will soon add photographs of the parade celebrating the NCAA national champions. Coach Dawn Staley has not only developed a winning team, but she has created a huge fan base that spreads a lot of love. They shake our hands or "high five," and only on rare occasions do our loyal fans "coach" the referees.

One highlight of the men's basketball collection is a framed photograph of our fans storming the floor, followed by our president, on January 26, 2010, when we beat Kentucky 68–62! Trust me, you can almost hear the crowd when you look at the picture! Recently we were excited to add memorabilia from their first NCAA Final Four appearance in 2017. With Frank Martin as coach, it won't be their last.

The crowd at the Statehouse following the parade honoring the 2017 NCAA Women's Basketball Championship team.
PHOTOGRAPH BY TRAVIS BELL.

We have two lovely posters of our women's golf team, one from the 2010 NCAA East Regional Championship and one from 2012 NCAA Eastern Regional Championship. The women visited at the President's House and personally delivered these mementos.

There is a commemorative soccer ball from 2009, when the women won the SEC and played in the NCAA Sweet Sixteen. They won the 2011 SEC Championship against Florida as well. And recently they added the 2016 SEC Championship to their titles.

The room is covered wall-to-wall with wonderful Gamecock memories, and filling in the spaces between are photographs of our fans—some people we know and some we've never met—all with big smiles and that never-say-die Gamecock spirit.

The only way to improve the "man cave" would be to pipe in "Sandstorm"!

The President's House greenhouse. PHOTOGRAPH BY KEITH MCGRAW.

❧ The Garden and the Greenhouse

As beautiful as the interior of the President's House is, the garden, greenhouse, and vegetable garden beckon me. There is a serenity in nature that is the perfect antidote to a busy, event-filled life. The songbirds, the rustling of leaves in the breeze, the shower of petals, and the fragrance of jasmine and tea olive all contribute to the Eden that is the President's House garden. Harris and I have quiet weekend meals in the garden, where we slip into our seats and watch the show unfold around us. Robins boisterously bathe in the fountain, or squirrels chase each other, jumping from one tree to the next. One of my favorite scenes was a family of mourning doves: the parents played in the fountain while all six chicks sat dutifully on the back of one bench.

Honeybees and hummingbirds are regular visitors, as are little green lizards (anoles). My young niece squeals when our horticulturist hangs one from his ear lobe.

While garden animals are quite innocuous in the botanical garden, it's a whole different story in the vegetable garden. We have grown vegetables for nine years now and have never had much trouble with squirrels until recently. I think it took them that long to realize there were more food options on campus than acorns and stray French fries. The

The antebellum kitchen and slave quarters, circa 1840, behind the President's House. PHOTOGRAPH BY KEITH MCGRAW.

winter of 2015 was particularly bad. We lost all the broccoli, cauliflower, and brussels sprouts. We were left with only kale, which apparently they don't care for.

I watch the figs like a hawk as soon as they begin to ripen, sometimes checking them twice a day. I'm willing to share the bounty, but it's heartbreaking to find tens of plump figs, each with one perfect hole pecked into it.

Once in a while we catch an animal doing something naughty, and we have to laugh. That was the case one summer when we witnessed a squirrel that had gotten hold of a tomato about half its size. The squirrel couldn't carry the large tomato, so it pushed it along the brick walk on its escape.

Over the years our "work family" has thoughtfully celebrated our birthdays with gifts that make the garden feel like our own. We received three different citrus trees, a pomegranate tree, a plum tree, and heirloom rosebushes. We've also received a fire pit and backyard games, which provide hours of enjoyment during family visits.

Having some privacy in the President's House garden is essential to the eventful life in the President's House. The care with which the grounds are beautifully maintained by Charlie Ryan and his team is a gift.

Just behind the President's House is the last remaining antebellum kitchen and slave quarters on the campus, built in the 1840s by Thomas Wade. Though other such buildings were demolished to make way for parking lots or new construction, this one was preserved because it was in continuous use. A 1937 article states that the McKissicks had completely renovated "the slave quarters so it would be 'in good order for books and use as study rooms.'" As a result, it became known as "Rion's Den." In 1946 it was renovated again to house the WUSC radio station.

Today the first floor is divided into two sections. One part has a partial dirt floor and houses mechanical equipment for the President's House. The other section is used as a lunchroom and office for the garden staff. The second floor is one large room, which is used as an office for the chief horticulturist and a storage room for the President's House.

Since the President's House garden has three distinct sections, we can use some or all of the garden depending on the number of guests. The large brick patio of the lower garden is surrounded by lush vegetation. Crape myrtle, loquat, holly fern, hydrangea, and loropetalum provide the foundation, and pots changed with the seasons feature plumbago as topiary, citrus fruit trees, olive trees, abutilon, and pinecone ginger. We can seat 100 there for dinner.

The middle garden is a large grassy yard bordered on one side by an arbor covered in Confederate jasmine and on the other side by large trees such as dogwood, flowering apricot, and crape myrtles. Interspersed with the trees are shrubs including azaleas and several different varieties of hydrangea. Lenten roses, Lady Banks roses, and peonies also grace the gardens. (I know peonies are not supposed to like the South, but we've had some limited success!) For seasonal color we often plant tulip and daffodil bulbs for early spring, impatiens for summer, mums for fall, and pansies for winter.

The upper garden has both brick and grassy sections and provides a more intimate seating area for smaller groups of guests. In the colder months we enjoy having evening fires in a portable fire pit.

Members of the 2012 football team toasting marshmallows with their president in the upper garden. PHOTOGRAPH BY KEITH MCGRAW.

A Present Past, fresco by Taylor Tynes in the President's House garden. PHOTOGRAPH BY KEITH MCGRAW.

Above and below: Details from the fresco. PHOTOGRAPHS BY KEITH MCGRAW.

❧ The Fresco: *A Present Past*

During the summer of 2016 we experienced heightened excitement in the garden when Taylor Tynes, a new magna cum laude graduate with a B.F.A. in studio arts painting, received a Magellan grant to paint a fresco on the wall under the arbor in the middle garden.

Taylor wanted the fresco to meld into the surroundings and complement but not distract from the beautiful gardens. As she contemplated a theme, she returned again and again to the quotation from Ovid on the university seal: "Learning humanizes character and does not permit it to be cruel." She thought of the early philosophers and settled on a wall of statues that could evoke the motto's significance.

Each of the characters in the mural—Plato, Aristotle, and Athena—has a specific relevance. The Plato and Aristotle statues are an homage to the master fresco painters of the past. Much of Taylor's inspiration came from Italian fresco paintings, specifically *The School of Athens* by Raphael. In addition Plato and Aristotle represent the coexistence of divergent philosophies, something we encourage in the university learning environment. Athena, who holds a place on our university seal, represents wisdom and knowledge. In her outstretched hand she holds her owl.

Taylor incorporated other woodland creatures into the scene: a blue jay carrying a pearl earring (a tribute to Mrs. Jones), mourning doves, a squirrel, an eastern tiger swallowtail butterfly, and a robin—all of which are regular visitors to the garden. The president's garden vegetation is also depicted with a pomegranate tree taking center stage.

It took Taylor some time to title her masterpiece. Because she sees this artwork and its location as an example of history and modern culture colliding in one time and space, she ultimately decided on *A Present Past* as she believes the past is always present in our daily lives, and integral to the flourishing of learning at the university.

How the President's House Is Used Today

Throughout the academic year we host breakfasts, luncheons, and dinners for small groups of up to twelve people in the main dining room of the house.

Larger sit-down dinners, for up to forty people, are held in the reception room upstairs, and occasionally we host buffet dinners using the back dining room for the food tables and either the front dining room or tables in the garden for seating.

Another creative use of the reception room was to host an intimate "themed" dinner when internationally recognized opera director Günter Krämer lectured in the School of Music. Though the dinner was not large, we used the reception room to accommodate a tabletop shaped like a grand piano.

In the nicer weather we often use the garden for sit-down dinners with a less-formal, bucolic theme. The garden gives us space to have a long farm table in the middle, a bar on the

Above and facing page: The dining-room table set for the dinner honoring Darla Moore on the unveiling of her portrait at the Darla Moore School of Business. PHOTOGRAPHS BY KEITH MCGRAW.

Toast welcoming Mrs. Nirupama Rao, then Indian ambassador to the United States. PHOTOGRAPH BY KEITH MCGRAW.

patio, a buffet under the arbor, and after-dinner entertainment in the lower garden.

Because our university community is so large, most of the receptions we host are for 100 or more people. We can fit about 150 people comfortably in the public areas of the house: the first floor and the reception room on the second floor. For events that are larger than the house can accommodate, we use the garden. We have hosted receptions for up to 600 people using the house and garden together.

Günter Krämer (right) greeting guests at the reception in his honor. PHOTOGRAPH BY JASON AYER.

Grand piano tabletop set in the reception room. PHOTOGRAPH BY KEITH MCGRAW.

Table set for a Tuscan dinner in the garden. PHOTOGRAPH BY KEITH MCGRAW.

❧ Parties for Students

Every year we attempt to invite new student groups who may not have visited the President's House before. With such a large university, we always seek opportunities to host small groups of students, so they can enjoy a more personal interaction with their president. In truth we also enjoy meeting our students in this more intimate fashion so we can get to know them better. We have held such events with many athletic teams, living and learning communities, the Honors College and other scholar groups, as well as members of clubs and organizations on campus.

Women's Basketball

With several successful seasons, including SEC championships and a trip to the 2015 Final Four, the women's basketball team visited the President's House for a luncheon. Players, coaches, and the male practice team enjoyed a purely social afternoon with Harris and me.

Dawn Staley, whose birthday we celebrated that day, is a winner. Earning several Olympic gold medals for playing and coaching women's basketball, Coach Staley is at the top

Visiting with the women's basketball team in the library.
PHOTOGRAPH BY JASON AYER.

of her field. As women's coach at USC, she has recruited well and built team after team that wins games and draws crowds. In 2017 she achieved the ultimate—the NCAA national championship. When she first came to USC, she had a loyal following of approximately one hundred fans. Today women's basketball games consistently attract twelve thousand.

Posing with the women's basketball team outside the President's House. PHOTOGRAPH BY JASON AYER.

Coach Staley has also developed a nonprofit program called INNERSOLE to provide new sneakers to children in need. With corporate gifts and community support, it has expanded to "Educate My Sole," where shoes are the rewards for academic performance in low-performing schools. With an emphasis on reading achievement and partnerships throughout the state, the program has already distributed more than eight thousand pairs of shoes.

When I'm asked to meet female basketball recruits and their families with Harris, I tell them all the wonderful attributes of the university and then I tell them that if I were a player, I'd want to play for Coach Staley. She has proven herself to be an excellent player and coach and a caring and engaged community leader. She's the best in my book.

The USC Marching Band

We have hosted the USC Marching Band several times for dinner in the garden. I have shoeboxes full of thank-you notes from band members—375 students to be exact! I've often thought that sometime during my golden years I will read one per day to brighten my world. I figure it's an assurance of squeaking out at least a few extra years of life.

Harris and I with USC Marching Band members.
PHOTOGRAPH BY JASON AYER.

The Women's Volleyball Team and the Carolina Gents

One year, after we had invited the volleyball team for a Sunday afternoon visit, we decided to invite the Carolina Gents to entertain them. Bringing together athletes and artists, who might not otherwise meet, seemed unexpected and fun. The star of the afternoon was Luke Tanner, the then

The women's volleyball team with Luke Tanner, in front of Harris and me. Luke's father, Athletics Director Ray Tanner, is second from right. PHOTOGRAPH BY JASON AYER.

The Carolina Gents with Harris and me and Luke Tanner. PHOTOGRAPH BY JASON AYER.

University ambassadors touring the President's House. PHOTOGRAPH BY JASON AYER.

nine-year-old son of Athletics Director Ray Tanner, who felt right at home with the college students.

University Ambassadors

Annually Harris and I host the Presidential Ambassadors for holiday tea as thanks for their helping guests at most events in the President's House. Depending on the size of the event, some or all of the roughly twelve Presidential Ambassadors greet guests, distribute name tags, and give directions. They are impressive representatives of our student body. We enjoy sitting in the library and hearing their personal stories—the adventures and challenges of university life, family holiday plans, travel abroad, and postgraduation plans.

We also host the larger group of around one hundred University Ambassadors from which the Presidential Ambassadors are chosen. Because these students are selected each year to lead university tours for prospective students, Harris and I meet with them annually to discuss what's new on campus and share the things he and I are most excited about. We then take questions from them, which we joke feels a bit like being a guest on *Inside the Actors Studio*. It's an evening we look forward to.

We receive rave reviews of the ambassadors from families touring campus. We are often told that the student-led tour was a turning point in helping them decide to attend USC. Our ambassadors invest themselves in their university.

Their authentic love for USC shines through their tours. Our University Ambassadors engender the welcoming culture that can make a large major research university feel like a small college.

Trick or Treat

Celebrating Halloween at the President's House is arguably not the most presidential activity of the year, but it is one of the most fun. Letting our hair down, dressing up, and being silly with our students is good, old-fashioned fun. Our tradition includes parking the Mini Cooper in front of the house and filling it with treats: chocolate bars, trail mix, and apples. Over the years Harris's costumes have adhered to a sports theme. He has dressed up as a catcher and a football player among others. I've been a chef, a witch, and a ballet dancer.

One year after receiving an equestrian-style button-down-collared shirt with a large embroidered gamecock on the back, I decided to be an equestrian for Halloween. With the black shirt, black jeans, and riding boots, I thought all I needed was a western cowboy hat. I tried it all on but something was missing.

Most all the riders on our team have long pony tails, so I ran out and bought a 16-inch pony tail of my own. It was fabulous. I whipped it around all evening and felt like a teen again.

Harris and I with trick-or-treaters. PHOTOGRAPH BY JASON AYER.

Above and below: Faculty enjoying OPA! in the President's House garden. PHOTOGRAPHS BY JASON AYER.

❦ OPA! The All-Faculty Party

Every fall we host a party to which we invite all full-time faculty. For the first couple of years, we called the party "Food for Thought" and served interesting ethnic foods, but I felt the party was a little sedate. My goal for the all-faculty party was for folks to come together and kick up their heels, not just mingle with colleagues they already knew from their

respective departments. After *Greek Revival: Cooking for Life* was published in 2010, we decided to have "OPA!" a Greek-themed party. I worked with our chefs to have them prepare recipes from the book. We hired a bouzouki player and decorated the trees in the garden with tiny white lights similar to those one might find at a taverna on a Greek island. It worked. The party was enlivened with the music, which even encouraged a little dancing. We have since made OPA! our annual theme, and added a colorful troupe of Greek dancers (our students) to lead the way.

❧ Parents Weekend

From the welcome reception to the beach bash to the tailgate party and football game, the University of South Carolina hosts a memorable Parents Weekend, with approximately nine thousand participants. Parents are able to attend academic classes and social events, reconnecting with their students and learning about their new college home.

The reception with the University President and First Lady is a long-standing tradition that keeps us standing long with several hundred parents to greet. Parents Weekend, Awards Day, and Commencement are premier student-parent events for us. We enjoy meeting and greeting the families that will become part of the "forever to thee" fold.

One of many proudly displayed Gamecock ornaments.
PHOTOGRAPH BY JASON AYER.

A Parents Weekend reception. PHOTOGRAPHS BY JASON AYER.

The main, traditional Christmas tree in the President's House library. PHOTOGRAPH BY KEITH MCGRAW.

❧ Holiday Decorating

Immediately following Thanksgiving, the house is turned upside down. Furniture is removed from the living room to accommodate a large Christmas tree. Framed photographs of our family and visiting dignitaries are boxed up and in their places are crèche sets, candelabras, angels, a menorah for Hanukkah, and a Kwanzaa set.

I added the menorah and Kwanzaa set the first year of Harris's presidency because I wanted to include others' traditions in our holiday décor. Pine boughs and garlands, mistletoe, boxwood wreaths, and colorful fruits predominate in our festive decorations.

The traditional events of the holiday season have included the USC Women's Club holiday decorating luncheon, the University Associates party, the faculty and staff open house,

Hanukkah menorah and dreidel. PHOTOGRAPH BY KEITH MCGRAW.

Kwanzaa set: African fabric mat, candelabra, unity cup, and corn. PHOTOGRAPH BY KEITH MCGRAW.

Presidential ambassadors and members of the University Women's Club, who decorated the President's House for the holidays in 2014. PHOTOGRAPH BY KEITH MCGRAW.

The student-athlete tree, crowned with Cocky.
PHOTOGRAPH BY KEITH MCGRAW.

the student open house, the holiday reception for the President's Executive Council, the Horseshoe Society reception, the Presidential Ambassadors' tea, Cocky's Reading Express with the First Lady, the University Community Advisory Committee reception, the foundations holiday reception, and the Board of Trustees holiday dinner. All our holiday parties are held by mid-December. In addition we manage to attend university departmental parties and a few annual parties of friends. This is a busy time of year—which football season trains us for!

As you can imagine, it takes many people to decorate the house. Lisa Robinette, house manager, and Don Staley, presidential catering manager, seek inspiration from many design sources throughout the year in preparation for the holidays. Don usually acts as the architect of the design for holiday décor and Lisa the general contractor. The rest of the special-events team serves as the subcontractors. Horticulturist Charlie Ryan cuts an array of greenery from across the campus and sets up the trees. He and his team decorate the windows and doors. Then on a designated morning during the first week of December, members of the University Women's Club arrive, like elves, to help trim the tree, make bows for wreaths, and hang garland on the bannisters of both staircases. The morning concludes with lunch and a great deal of catching up, as I usually won't have seen them since the University Women's Club fall coffee to welcome new members. This soup and sandwich lunch with the ladies is something I look forward to each year as it designates the official beginning of our compressed holiday entertaining season. The lunch is the calm before the storm.

Just like my food choices, my preference for holiday décor is plant materials. We use fresh Frazier fir evergreen Christmas trees: a large one in the library and smaller ones in the back dining room and the hallway across from the guest closets. The primary tree in the library is traditional. The one or sometimes two small trees in the back dining room are used to display a holiday theme, and the one across from the coat closets has become a tradition of Harris's term, a student-athlete tree. It has glass ornaments representing various sports as well as stacks of books and diplomas. The concept for this tree came from Harris's Secret Santa, who recognized Harris's love of sport.

We use approximately forty-four poinsettias in an assortment of six-, eight-, and ten-inch pots to adorn the fireplaces, foyers, and tabletops. We also use some four-inch and two-inch mini poinsettias in dish gardens. In recent years we've purchased all white ones from three local family-owned companies. They're a greenish white, elegant and stately.

Having such a large number of poinsettias might seem wasteful, but they serve double duty. Because our holiday entertaining season ends by mid-December, we distribute the poinsettias as thank-you gifts to the many offices that support the President's House all through the school year.

We also have a longstanding tradition of using cut smilax in pots of water to embellish the large gilded mirrors in the foyer, dining room, and on the second-floor landing just outside the ballroom. Smilax (aka greenbrier) grows like a weed in South Carolina. Former horticulturist Fred Drafts used to pull it from trees on his parents' property in Lexington for our holiday decorating. After Fred passed away, as if by his hand, we noticed smilax growing in the President's House garden. To this day, we use the smilax that we believe Fred left us.

White poinsettias, a new favorite. PHOTOGRAPH BY KEITH MCGRAW.

The foyer with smilax adorning the mirror and greenery and poinsettias abounding. PHOTOGRAPH BY KEITH MCGRAW.

One of many crèche sets belonging to the President's House. PHOTOGRAPH BY KEITH MCGRAW.

Pearls add a fresh twist to a green theme. PHOTOGRAPH BY KEITH MCGRAW.

A library mantel sparkling with tiny lights. PHOTOGRAPH BY KEITH MCGRAW.

The two mantelpieces in the library are bedecked with Leyland cypress, cryptomeria, assorted pine, and holly. Recently we used moss-covered Oasis to create a lush forest floor, to which we added ripe red pomegranates and shiny gold balls, bookended by ivy topiaries ringed with tiny succulents.

Traditional evergreen garlands drape the bannisters and frame the doorways. The fragrance of the President's House at Christmas is undeniably fresh pine.

Overleaves:

Our current décor highlights the new neutrals of the library with a range of muted aqua, gold, and ivory, creating a sea of calm during a hectic season. PHOTOGRAPH BY KEITH MCGRAW.

The red maple tree setting off the Christmas greenery on the exterior of the President's House. PHOTOGRAPH BY KEITH MCGRAW.

Cocky's Reading Express at the President's House

I'm proud of the many ways our students give back to our community. In December 2005 soon-to-be student body president Tommy Preston entered the charge to fight illiteracy in South Carolina by creating Cocky's Reading Express (CRE).

As part of CRE, USC students visit elementary schools and read to the children in the younger grades. These volunteers bring along our mascot Cocky, who doesn't speak but acts out the stories as they are read. The children are then asked to promise Cocky that they will read every day. To be certain they have something to read, Cocky gives each child a book or two to keep.

Every CRE visit is a touching and sweet encounter. The little ones are generally excited to meet Cocky, although an occasional child is frightened at first by this massive furry, garnet rooster. Our students often select books that were their favorites growing up and read them with great enthusiasm. Tommy remembers one small boy who approached him after he read to the class and asked if he was "real." Did he think Tommy was a character like Cocky? Or perhaps the child had no men in his life who read to him. One can only imagine the impact this program has on all involved.

I've gone to some schools with CRE and read with classrooms of children. They can't take their eyes off Cocky, and he often incites riotous laughter and good cheer. The line is drawn very clearly, however, if the teacher suggests a class picture with Cocky. There are usually a couple of children who declare themselves Clemson Tigers and step away from the photo op! They certainly identify young here in South Carolina!

It gives me great personal pleasure to invite a local kindergarten class into the President's House for CRE at holiday time. One year the four-year-old kindergarten class from St. Martin de Porres School visited. They looked very spiffy in their uniforms. I don't know the last time I saw school children wearing leather shoes. As they were leaving one little girl complimented the President's House, saying, "This is the kind of house I'd like to live in when I grow up." I answered, "Keep reading and one day you may *be* the university president!"

USC Child Development Center students enjoying Cocky. PHOTOGRAPH BY JASON AYER.

❧ The Board of Trustees
Annual Holiday Dinner

One of the more formal dinners we host annually is the holiday dinner for the USC Board of Trustees. University trustees spend something on the order of 150 hours of meetings annually in service to the university. There are six full board meetings yearly, and members typically serve on three standing committees each, which require four meetings per year. In addition, there have been as many as four ad hoc committees meetings at once. Trustees also attend a two day planning retreat each year and are expected to attend as many commencements as possible and support many special events. University trustees attend the President's State of the University address, Carolina Day at the Statehouse, lecture series, donor events, special recognitions, and arts and athletic events. We view the holiday dinner as a time to thank them with a specially selected multicourse dinner in the elegant ballroom of the president's home. The evening begins with cocktails on the first floor, so they can stroll through the house, socialize, and enjoy the decorations.

After welcoming everyone we are entertained by a group of student singers. Over the years we've enjoyed several a cappella groups: female, male, and coed. One year we had just been informed by Pam Bowman, director of USC Special Events, that none of the a cappella groups was available to perform at our holiday events because of their exam schedules. We were disappointed, but, as Harris and I stepped out the front door heading to an event at the McKissick Museum, we were delighted to meet a group of about forty students who had come caroling. We invited them in to see the decorations, and they stood in two rows, shoulder to shoulder before the Christmas tree and sang for us. I became tearful at the beauty of their harmonies and the sentiments of the season. Until then I hadn't stopped long enough to feel the joy of Christmas. They were so talented that I asked if these young men and women might be free to sing for us again during the season, and they agreed to check their calendars. That is how the students of Phi Mu Alpha and Kappa Kappa Psi, two musical fraternities, came to perform at the Board of Trustees dinner and brought tears to more eyes than just mine.

Prior to ascending to the ballroom for dinner, the trustees bestow a Christmas gift on us. Thanks to the thoughtful generosity of the USC Board of Trustees, we now have two matching University of South Carolina children's rocking chairs with our granddaughters' names on them.

After we are all seated in the ballroom, our dinner commences with a prayer. I often joke that, while Harris and I have always prayed, this job has caused us to pray *together*. To lead a community of 48,355 students, 2,390 full-time faculty, and 4,028 full-time staff is to experience the greatest happiness and the deepest sadness of human life. We have found shared morning prayer the best way to be centered and mindful, whatever the day may bring. At holiday dinners and many other events at the house, Harris asks me to pray, and I find great joy in sharing words that are uplifting, inclusive, and meaningful to the event.

I've work closely with our food-service provider since 2008 to plan memorable dinners. For special events such as the trustees dinner and the commencement dinner, the presidential chef and I plan a menu and have a tasting weeks prior to the event. The tasting allows us to tweak the menu for added color or enhanced local ingredients, and we also select wine pairings. Here is a sample dinner card for a dinner prepared by Chef Peter Zoellinger:

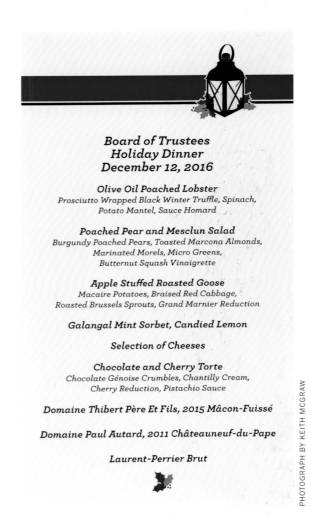

**Board of Trustees
Holiday Dinner
December 12, 2016**

Olive Oil Poached Lobster
Prosciutto Wrapped Black Winter Truffle, Spinach,
Potato Mantel, Sauce Homard

Poached Pear and Mesclun Salad
Burgundy Poached Pears, Toasted Marcona Almonds,
Marinated Morels, Micro Greens,
Butternut Squash Vinaigrette

Apple Stuffed Roasted Goose
Macaire Potatoes, Braised Red Cabbage,
Roasted Brussels Sprouts, Grand Marnier Reduction

Galangal Mint Sorbet, Candied Lemon

Selection of Cheeses

Chocolate and Cherry Torte
Chocolate Génoise Crumbles, Chantilly Cream,
Cherry Reduction, Pistachio Sauce

Domaine Thibert Père Et Fils, 2015 Mâcon-Fuissé

Domaine Paul Autard, 2011 Châteauneuf-du-Pape

Laurent-Perrier Brut

Tables set for a Board of Trustees holiday dinner.
PHOTOGRAPH BY KEITH MCGRAW.

Harris is a creative person, and he started a tradition in 2008 of writing an annual version of "The Twelve Days of Christmas." The lyrics satirize the past year's challenges within the university and the board's expectations for him. For example, when the board enthusiastically debated USC's growth trajectory, Harris characterized their charge as "to grow and shrink enrollment!" At the conclusion of the holiday dinner, Harris and I sing his "Twelve Days of Christmas," which ends the evening on a high (occasionally flat) note!

As our guests depart, they receive two gifts that have become a tradition—a donation in their name to a university department or program that they personally care about and a small gift that I've chosen, usually something for the table. Tableware resonates with me as a symbol of home and hospitality, which is perhaps the most enduring tradition of the President's House.

Table decorations for a Board of Trustees dinner.
PHOTOGRAPH BY KEITH MCGRAW.

Student carolers from Phi Mu Alpha and Kappa Kappa Psi. PHOTOGRAPH BY KEITH MCGRAW.

Harris and I awaiting our guests for a trustees holiday dinner.
PHOTOGRAPH BY KEITH MCGRAW.

—and receiving a personalized USC rocker for Alice Anastasia,
granddaughter number two. PHOTOGRAPH BY KEITH MCGRAW.

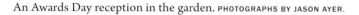
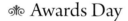

An Awards Day reception in the garden. PHOTOGRAPHS BY JASON AYER.

❧ Awards Day

Every April the university hosts Awards Day on the Horse-shoe. The academic accomplishments of hundreds of students from all departments are recognized. The top graduating seniors receive the Steven N. Swanger Leadership Award, for exemplary leadership and significant contributions to the university community, and the Algernon Sydney Sullivan Awards, for the male and female seniors with outstanding achievements in campus leadership, exemplary character, and service to the community. The ceremonies culminate with a reception for all awardees and their family members in the President's House gardens, where graduating seniors have the opportunity to take photographs with the president.

Faculty feted at the 2015 authors' party. PHOTOGRAPHS BY JASON AYER.

❧ Faculty Authors, March 2, 2015

Every two years we host a reception for faculty members who have published new books. This stimulating event showcases the work of our exceptional faculty and gives Harris and me an opportunity to fete them for their accomplishments. This is one of my favorite parties because the guest list includes a "mere" ninety or so faculty, giving us the opportunity to spend more time talking with each guest than at the all-faculty party, where we sometimes host upwards of five hundred. In 2015 we welcomed almost one hundred new titles to our library, including fourteen from the English department, eleven from the languages, literatures, and cultures department, ten from history, and ten from music. We hold a few shelves in the center of the library, where we keep these new books for our guests to peruse.

With the expert attention of house manager Lisa Robinette, housekeeper Joyce Taylor, and horticulturist Charles Ryan, the house and garden receive periodic maintenance as well as daily care. For being 163 years old the President's House is stately and aging well! As a venue for university events, the President's House is historic and formally appointed, but also warm and comfortable. It's a place we are honored to call home and to welcome the Gamecock faithful.

Housekeeper Joyce Taylor, horticulturist Charlie Ryan, and house manager Lisa Robinette.
PHOTOGRAPH BY KEITH MCGRAW.

Highlights of My Time in the President's House

The official investiture. PHOTOGRAPH BY KEITH MCGRAW.

A moment of pride for me. PHOTOGRAPH BY KEITH MCGRAW.

So many things have happened during my ten years in the President's House. I've selected a few of the highlights to share.

❧ November 21, 2008: Investiture of the Twenty-eighth President

I can't imagine ever looking back on our time in the President's House without remembering the unadulterated pride I felt at Harris's investiture. Our family members and lifelong friends traveled to Columbia for the occasion, largely from New York and New England.

On their arrival we hosted a southern barbeque dinner for them catered by Sue Hodges of the Happy Café. That meal won over all hearts, and her caramel cake seduced a few to aspire to the status of so-called Damn Yankees (the kind that don't want to go back north).

My brothers John and Robert represented their alma maters, Wesleyan and Quinnipiac Universities, in the colorful procession of academics from dozens of universities. My cousin Col. Richard Coleman wore his U.S. Marine Corps dress uniform. The Honorable Miles Loadholt presided over the installation, and Dr. Robert Blocker, the Henry and Lucy Moses Dean of Music at Yale University, provided a heartfelt and personal keynote address. I sat beside the chair of the Faculty Senate, Dr. Robert Best, and watched as the university medallion was placed on Harris's shoulders. The ceremony was moving. The weight of Harris's deceased parents' absence was daunting for a moment, but as Harris spoke with passion of his vision for the university, I felt them beaming.

Because of the economic recession, we held a light reception after the ceremony and a smaller formal party at the President's House in the evening. I was initially disappointed to relinquish the traditional dinner dance, not so much for the dinner as the dance—but when that evening came, I was floating on air, dance or none.

OCTOBER 29, 2008: LUNCH AT THE WAGON WHEEL, LANCASTER, S.C.

Not long before his investiture, Harris and I enjoyed a fabulous Greek lunch at the Wagon Wheel restaurant in Lancaster, South Carolina, with then trustee James Bradley. Mr. Bradley imparted these words of wisdom to the new president:

RULES FOR SUCCESS

To succeed one must possess:
  A willingness to work hard
  The mentality to work smart
  An adequate amount of commonsense
  Good communications skills
  The right balance between patience and impatience!

With our children, Katharine and Andrew, at the evening celebration. PHOTOGRAPH BY KEITH MCGRAW.

❧ August 8, 2008: Gus Speth, Sustainability, and Our First Commencement Dinner

In the fall of 2007 Harris and I attended a conference at Yale on the topic of Yale in a Green World. The keynote speaker was Gus Speth, then dean of the Yale School of Forestry and Environmental Studies. In addition to his work to protect the environment nationally he was instrumental in developing programs to encourage sustainability at Yale. As we listened,

President Pastides looking on as honorary-degree recipient Gus Speth receives a print of the Horseshoe by artist Blue Sky from student body president Andrew Gaeckle and Ashley Wood, president of Carolina Productions, August 2008. PHOTOGRAPH BY KEITH MCGRAW.

The Arnold School of Public Health research center set for the August 2008 commencement dinner.
PHOTOGRAPH BY KEITH MCGRAW.

he spoke of growing up on the Edisto River in South Carolina, and our ears perked up. We were so impressed with him and all he'd accomplished at Yale that we shared the same thought: we need to bring him back to his home state with his powerful message of sustainability. One of the initiatives he discussed, which interested me, was how Yale evaluated the amount of food students were wasting. When allowed to control their own portions with buffet-style dining, they often took too much food, and what they didn't eat was discarded. Yale did away with the self-serve buffet line. Instead fixed portions were served to students, who were welcome to return for seconds if they were still hungry. Savings were substantial.

When we returned to South Carolina, Harris nominated Dr. Speth for an honorary degree, which was bestowed on him at our first commencement, the eighth day of Harris's presidency. It was an honor to entertain Dr. Speth, his wife, Cameron, and several of his family members at the President's House. The connection between the Speths and Harris's former role as dean of the Norman J. Arnold School of Public Health led us to host the commencement dinner at the then-new Arnold public health research center. We were pleased to be able to point out the flooring made of recycled materials, and the Silver LEED standard to which the building had been constructed. (LEED stands for "Leadership in Energy and Environmental Design," an organization that certifies green buildings.) Somehow the special events staff, led by Pamela Bowman, turned the academic venue into a wonderland, the first of many beautiful events they have organized for us.

Dr. Speth—scientist, educator, and South Carolinian— was an inspiration. He opened my eyes to the need for infusing all university endeavors with a conscious promotion of sustainability. With the Speths' visit, I began to think about how the President's House is used, particularly because we have so many events that can create a huge carbon footprint. In addition to using more biodegradable materials, recycling more effectively, and growing our own vegetables sustainably, we focus our attention on creating carbon offsets. These are initiatives that actually put more oxygen into the environment, such as planting trees. Every year we plant two or more new trees around the garden. And it's been fun to create gifts such as herb gardens in recycled olive-oil cans. Concern for sustainability carries over to decorating the house with potted plants and dish gardens so we can use fewer cut flowers. When we do purchase cut flowers, we reuse them for several events, refrigerating them between uses to promote their longevity. We continue to seek opportunities to become an ever-more sustainable community. Over the years we've worked closely with Sustainable Carolina to support initiatives in pursuit of this goal.

Fred Drafts and I donating organically grown vegetables from the President's House garden to Kim Johnson of Harvest Hope Food Bank and the Reverend Darryl Brooks of Good Shepherd Church in Hopkins, South Carolina. PHOTOGRAPH BY MIKE BROWN.

❧ October 13, 2009: Making It Grow in the Garden

The very first thing I told host Roland Alston when he invited me to be his guest on the ETV program *Making It Grow* was that I didn't actually make it grow. Fred Drafts made it grow. But Roland still wanted to tape an episode of his program at the house and in the garden, so I agreed that Fred and I would show him around, and I would prepare lunch from the garden for him and his staff.

As soon as the camera started rolling, Roland announced, "Patricia Moore-Pastides is First Lady of the University of South Carolina and a *master gardener.*" Yikes. I blushed, sure that my lack of horticultural experience would betray me

instantly. I recovered with the earnest protest, "I don't make it grow, I make it food," and the show went on. I prepared a Greek salad, Imam Baildi, and Lemon and Oregano Roasted Potatoes for lunch. Roland, who is part Lebanese, was familiar with Mediterranean foods, and I was much more relaxed chatting about the food preparation. The best part was that the majority of the ingredients were from our new organic vegetable garden, and though I couldn't take a mustard seed's worth of responsibility for growing them, I was proud to serve them. That spring, after the school year ended and our event schedule wound down, we dug up the remainder of the potatoes and onions and were able to donate ninety pounds to Harvest Hope Food Bank.

❧ Mr. Mooneyhan and His Heirloom Seeds

The vegetable garden at the President's House captivated many people, one of whom was a ninety-one-year-old man named James Mooneyhan. His daughter called to tell me he had heirloom seeds he'd saved for years and wanted to send some to me so I could cultivate good old-fashioned southern vegetables, unadulterated by genetic modification. This was a new concept to me at the time, but I was interested in the prospect of recovering taste and nutrition through growing vegetables such as "ugly tomatoes."

When Mr. Mooneyhan's daughter, Barbara, dropped off the seeds, she happened to mention that her father lived in a nursing home. I remember telling her, "Barbara, if these heirloom seeds take off, we'll spring your father from the nursing home to come for a visit."

And that's just what we did. On July 31, 2009, I had the sweetest visit in the President's House with Mr. Mooneyhan, who explained that he had been a seed tester on James Island, South Carolina, for a seed catalog. He received seeds, planted them, and wrote descriptions of the plants as they grew. He then sent his accounts back to the company and

One of the vegetable plants grown from Mr. Mooneyhan's seeds.
PHOTOGRAPH BY KEITH MCGRAW.

waited excitedly for the catalogs to arrive, hoping he would find himself published.

During our visit, on the eve of his ninety-second birthday, we walked through the garden. I was able to show him cow-horn okra, red civi beans, and the start of several ugly tomatoes that were the best I ever tasted.

Mr. James Mooneyhan and I among his heirloom crops at the President's House vegetable garden.
PHOTOGRAPH BY KEITH MCGRAW.

Fred Drafts and I proudly displaying our first cabbage.
PHOTOGRAPH BY KEITH MCGRAW.

❧ October 20, 2010: The Fred Drafts Memorial Service

I suppose it's not surprising when you live at your workplace, that the people you work with become your "work family." That was the case with Fred Drafts, who was chief horticulturist at the President's House from 1997 to 2010. He had a debilitating illness, which left him in a continuously weakening state; yet he worked up until the day he died, May 21, 2010. I was not at home that day, but I was told he was too weak to walk, so he rolled himself around the brick path of the garden on a desk chair and barked orders at his team.

I know Fred had a good rapport with the two First Ladies who preceded me in the President's House, Mrs. Palms and Mrs. Sorensen. When I met him, I found him to be quiet and felt I had to draw him out. I imagined he was thinking "now I have to get used to yet another 'lady of the garden!'" I like to think I wore him down because I stopped and talked with him whenever he was in sight. He noticed I made a habit of cutting herbs to use in my cooking, and he approached me one day with a question that altered my life at the President's House in many ways:

"How would you like to have a vegetable garden?"

I had never given it any consideration, but I answered without hesitation: "Yes, if it can be organic!" And we were off and running, collaborators on a new adventure.

What a generous man Fred was. To propose a new project that would require him and his team to work harder broke the stereotype of government employees. It was a completely selfless act on his part. He knew instinctively I would relish having a vegetable garden, and he made it happen.

The last time I spoke to Freddie he looked very thin and was bent nearly in half over his cane. I knew he didn't have much of an appetite, but I ran into the house and produced a bowl of strawberry shortcake with Callie's biscuits (of Charleston), organic, ripe, red, juicy strawberries, and freshly whipped cream. I brought it to him, saying, "Freddie, eat this, it will fix you right up." We stood in the garden house for a moment, and as I was on my way out, I paused and said, "Fred, I just want you to know that I love you." And he said he loved me too. Those were our last words. I learned later from staff that, during the course of that day, he'd eaten every last bite of the strawberry shortcake.

I have since recognized Fred's presence on many occasions when I'm in the garden—through the sudden appearance of butterflies and dragonflies or when I sit on the teak bench that bears a plaque urging: "Pause here and enjoy the peace and beauty of the garden Fred cultivated and cherished."

My favorite tale of Fred's spirit is that in life he ate every vegetable, *swimming* in olive oil, I ever prepared for him, except eggplant. He just disliked it, Mediterranean or not. He grew a few plants that produced a modest yield, but after his death eggplants took off like crazy in the yard, and whenever I cut them I could hear: "Now that I'm gone you can have as many as you like."

My prayer for Fred at his memorial service was more a prayer in Fred's voice for those of us left behind, including his parents, siblings, cousins, friends, and many work family members.

The words are from *Prayers for a Planetary Pilgrim* by Edward Hays from his "Psalm for the Dying":

Relatives and friends, I am about to leave;
My last breath does not say "good-bye,"
For my love for you is truly timeless,
Beyond the touch of boney death.
I leave myself not to the undertaker,
For decoration in his house of the dead,
But to your memory, with love.
I leave my thoughts, my laughter, my dreams
To you, whom I have treasured
Beyond gold and precious gems.
I give you what no thief can steal,
the memories of our times together:
the tender, love-filled moments,
the success we have shared,
the hard times that brought us closer together
and the roads we have walked side by side.
I also leave you a solemn promise
that after I am home in the bosom of God,

I will still be present,
whenever and wherever you call on me.
My energy will be drawn to you
by the magnet of our love.
Whenever you are in need, call me
I will come to you,
With my arms full of wisdom and light
To open up your blocked paths,
To untangle your knots
And to be your avenue to God.
And all I take with me as I leave
Is your love and the millions of memories
Of all that we have shared.
So I truly enter my new life as a millionaire.
Fear not, nor grieve at my departure,
You whom I have loved so much
For my roots and yours are forever intertwined.

In memory of
Fred L. Drafts
President's House Horticulturalist
1997–2010

Pause here and enjoy the peace and beauty
of the garden Fred cultivated and cherished.

Fred's special corner of the President's House garden. PHOTOGRAPHS BY KEITH MCGRAW.

The 2013 fashion show and auction to benefit the USC Center for Colon Cancer Research. PHOTOGRAPH BY KEITH MCGRAW.

✂ Center for Colon Cancer Research Fund-Raisers

As one might expect, the majority of our time is devoted to raising money to support the important work of our faculty and students. Colon cancer is a serious health issue, and we have an active Center for Colon Cancer Research (CCCR) under the expert direction of Dr. Frank Berger.

While fashion and academics might seem an incongruous pairing, they converged in the life of Carmen Marc Valvo, a highly respected clothing designer who is also a colon-cancer survivor. CCCR reached out to Mr. Valvo some years ago, and he has generously given of his time, talents, and treasure on several occasions in support of community

Harris and I with Carmen Marc Valvo in the President's House garden, 2010. PHOTOGRAPH BY COURTNEY DOX.

Bruce Greenberg, Anne Sinclair, Josanne Wilson, Dr. Frank Berger, me, Harris, Kendra McBride, and Dr. March Seabrook. PHOTOGRAPH BY KEITH MCGRAW.

education and the research projects of the center. I enjoy fabrics, colors, and styles and view fashion as a form of artistic expression, so with great enthusiasm, we hosted—not our typical reception—but a fashion show featuring Carmen's designs in the ballroom of the President's House.

The ballroom became the runway with two rows of chairs on either side. Bruce and Sherri Greenberg provided the beautiful ensembles from Coplon's, their women's clothing store. Bruce and Sherri have been generous supporters of the CCCR and USC Dance as well. In addition to the fashion show we conducted an auction that included a highly sought after trip to New York City for Fashion Week and a Healthy Mediterranean Cooking Class for twelve.

I offered the cooking class, which was held months later at Columbia's Cooking, part of the University's Cancer Prevention and Control Program, where community cooking classes are tools for healthier lifestyles.

The CCCR fund-raiser was profitable and fun and proved, in case there should be any doubt, that fashion and academics are not mutually exclusive.

❧ My Strangest Encounter with a Student

I should probably begin this tale by saying that life on a university campus is truly wonderful. No two days are the same. The students have not yet lost their spirit of play, and many are fearless in the best sense of the word. The energy they bring to this community is palpable. We wait impatiently for their return in August because a campus without a full complement of students is too quiet, a little dusty and lifeless. I have seen Harris bound out of the front door to greet a tour group or take pictures with students on their way to a formal, and it restores him to be among them. We love our students, even when an occasional misguided act reminds us that their frontal lobes are still developing.

Late one afternoon I was heading out the back door of the house into the parking enclosure to go to the visitation for Trustee Michael Mungo, who died April 11, 2010, after serving as a trustee for thirty-seven years. The backdoor landing is the height of a truck bed to accommodate catering deliveries to the kitchen, so as I exited the building I could see over the tops of our cars, and I spied a young man with his back to me, apparently relieving himself on my herb garden. I shouted, "What do you think you're doing?" When he turned to respond, my car blocked his partial nudity from my view, but it was conveniently caught on the house security camera. He apologized for not knowing someone lived here. He just thought it was "state property," which apparently made it permissible to urinate on. With further questioning I learned he was a fifth-year senior, one who wasn't aware of the locations of bathrooms on the Horseshoe! Since he gave me his real name (he had integrity after all), I reported the incident, and he was called to the student judicial council.

Since he admitted the offense, no viewing of the videotape was necessary, and I was asked to weigh in on his punishment. The students had recommended cleaning toilets, but seeing no malicious intent I requested that he write me a letter of apology. He wrote a very formal letter assuring me that his parents had not reared him to behave in such poor taste and ending with "even though it was under such unusual circumstances, it was still an honor to meet you." At the suggestion of the faculty liaison to student judiciary, he included two packs of herb seeds.

I dropped his letter into the archive box so someone one day will have a chuckle while sorting through the more typical President's House correspondence.

Katharine, Penelope, and Papou on Penelope's first birthday.
PHOTOGRAPH BY KEITH MCGRAW.

❧ April 2013, 2015, and 2017:
   Penelope's Birthday Parties

Penelope Jean Erickson, daughter of Katharine Pastides Erickson and Forest Erickson, paid a visit to her grandparents on her first birthday, April 29, 2013. Her first cupcake was the highlight of the celebration. Our thoughts on grandparenthood: it is definitely not overrated!

In April 2015, Penelope spent her third birthday at the President's House, this time with her fifteen-month-old sister, Alice Anastasia. (They got to actually play in the playroom on the sun porch, rather than virtually on FaceTime.) They also loved the backyard, where running and hiding were top priorites. For Penelope's third birthday, Lisa Robinette created a three-year-old's version of a prom. Penelope was thrilled. In 2017 we had a dinosaur party.

Penelope and Alice in the playroom wearing dresses made by USC alumna Annabelle LaRoque. PHOTOGRAPH BY KEITH MCGRAW.

Nothing like the first taste of cake! PHOTOGRAPH BY KEITH MCGRAW.

Alice and Penelope "racing" their rocking chairs. PHOTOGRAPH BY KEITH MCGRAW.

Above and right: Penelope's third birthday party.
PHOTOGRAPHS BY KEITH MCGRAW.

Penelope's fifth birthday and Alice's "unbirthday."
PHOTOGRAPHS BY KEITH MCGRAW.

❧ October 31, 2013: The Investiture of the McCausland Faculty Fellows

Peter and Bonnie McCausland have long been generous donors to the University of South Carolina, Peter's alma mater. The endowment of the McCausland Faculty Fellows program is a valuable asset to the university. Exceptional faculty members, who are typically sought after by competing universities (and at times successfully "stolen"), are awarded supplemental grants for five years to conduct their research. This program rewards faculty members of the College of Arts and Sciences who are within ten years of having earned their doctoral degrees. It creates a powerful magnet for keeping talented professors at USC. The endowment will ultimately support twenty fellowships. On October 31, 2013, we celebrated the investiture of the first four McCausland Faculty Fellows: Dr. Hunter Harrington Gardner, Department of Languages, Literatures, and Cultures; Dr. Blaine David Griffen, Biological Sciences and Marine Science; Dr. Katherine Elizabeth Keyser, Department of English Language and Literature; and Dr. Joseph Adam November, Department of History. The ceremony was held in Rutledge Chapel followed by a dinner in the reception room at the President's House.

Don Staley and Bonnie McCausland looking over the autumn table decorations, which included folk-art pottery from Pennsylvania. PHOTOGRAPH BY KEITH MCGRAW.

Harris toasting the McCauslands at the dinner in their honor. PHOTOGRAPH BY KEITH MCGRAW.

❧ September 11, 2013: Fiftieth Anniversary of Desegregation Luncheon

On September 11, 1963, Henrie Monteith, James L. Solomon Jr., and Robert G. Anderson became the first African American students to be allowed to enroll at the University of South Carolina since 1877. Black students were allowed to enroll after the Civil War, but the college was closed in 1877 and reopened as an all-white institution in 1880. With careful consideration of how to best commemorate the fiftieth anniversary of desegregation of the university, a committee of faculty, administrators, alumni, and community leaders scheduled a year of public events. The university sought to honor the three students, express its commitment to making the university accessible to all, and "educate, enrich, challenge and inspire" citizens of all ages through lectures, art exhibits, and performances. And what a year it was. We learned about civil rights struggles from Andrew Young and Diane Nash, and our undergraduates presented their own research on the African American experience at USC. Our students and faculty presented original musical compositions and choreography during the final commemorative event, which we called "Our Journey Forward."

The first of two highlights for me was "Retracing Our Steps," the premiere event held on September 11, 2013, fifty years to the day of official desegregation. It featured a symbolic walk up the stairs to the Osborne Administration Building by Dr. Monteith Treadwell and Mr. Solomon. Mr. Robert G. Anderson had passed away, but I think we all felt his presence there with us. The second was the unveiling of the Desegregation Meditation Garden with a living sculpture—three topiaries created by Mr. Pearl Fryar—and a poem written for the occasion by Professor Nikky Finney and inscribed in granite in the garden:

Henrie Monteith Treadwell and James Solomon on the Osborne steps fifty years to the day after they desegregated the modern university. James Solomon is wearing a hat that belonged to the late Robert Anderson. PHOTOGRAPH BY JASON AYER.

The Irresistable Ones

ROBERT ANDERSON   HENRIE MONTEITH   JAMES SOLOMON

They arrive knocking at Osborne's great garnet door. They want to study mathematics, join the debate team, and sing in the choir. They are three in a sea of six thousand. With each step they pole vault shards of doubt, sticks of dynamite, and stubborn hate mail. With them arrives the bright peppermint of change. The new laws of the new day can no longer resist these three irresistible ones, in a sea of six thousand, stepping through a door now garnet and black.

Mr. and Mrs. James Solomon standing before Pearl Fryar's topiaries and Nikky Finney's "The Irresistible Ones."
PHOTOGRAPH BY JASON AYER.

After the opening ceremony, we hosted a lunch at the President's House for thirty-three guests, including Dr. Monteith Treadwell and Mr. Solomon and their families and Mr. Anderson's partner, Susan Raskin—as well as university and community leaders. I had been invited to say a prayer before the meal, and I thought deeply about how to pray in a manner that would respect the significance of this day. As a young girl during the civil rights movement, I watched the struggle playing out on the evening news. I was moved by the need for equality and horrified by what I witnessed on our small television. Though more than fifty years have now passed, our community is a microcosm of our country, where we still see episodes of mistrust, misunderstanding, and bigotry. Searching for just the right prayer was supremely important to me.

Fortunately our Methodist Student Network had given Harris and me *Guerrillas of Grace: Prayers for the Battle* by

Luncheon at the President's House to commemorate the fiftieth anniversary of desegregation. PHOTOGRAPH BY JASON AYER.

Ted Loder, and I found "Help Me to Believe in Beginnings" in a chapter called "Prayers for Commitment and Change." By changing the pronouns from singular to plural, I had just the prayer I needed:

> God of history and of our hearts,
> so much has happened to us during these
>   whirlwind days:
>   We've known death and birth;
>   We've been brave and scared;
>   We've hurt, we've helped;
>   We've been honest, we've lied;
>   We've destroyed, we've created;
>   We've been with people, we've been lonely;
>   We've been loyal, we've betrayed;
>   We've decided, we've waffled;
>   We've laughed and we've cried.
> You know our frail hearts and our frayed history—
> And now another day begins.

Bricks added to the historic Horseshoe to recognize the first African American students admitted to the modern university.
PHOTOGRAPH BY JASON AYER.

> Oh God, help us to believe in beginnings
> and in our beginning again,
> no matter how often we have failed before.
>
> Help us to make beginnings:
>   to begin going out of our weary minds into fresh
>   dreams,
>   daring to make our own bold tracks in the land
>   of now;
>   to begin forgiving
>   that we may experience mercy;
>   to begin questioning the unquestionable
>   that we may know truth;
>   to begin disciplining
>   that we may create beauty;
>   to begin sacrificing
>   that we may accomplish justice;
>   to begin risking
>   that we may make peace;
>   to begin loving
>   that we may realize joy.
>
> Help us to be a beginning to others,
>   to be singers to the songless,
>   storytellers to the aimless,
>   befrienders of the friendless,
> to become a beginning of hope for the despairing,
>   of assurance for the doubting,
>   of reconciliation for the divided;
> to become a beginning of freedom for the oppressed,
>   of comfort for the sorrowing,
>   of friendship for the forgotten;
> to become a beginning of beauty for the forlorn,
>   of sweetness for the soured,
>   of gentleness for the angry,
>   of wholeness for the broken,
>   of peace for the frightened and violent of the earth.
>
> Help us to believe in beginnings,
>   to make a beginning,
>   to be a beginning,
> so that we may not just grow old,
>   but grow new
> each day of this wild, amazing life
>   you call us to live. . . .

September 30, 2013: Installation of the Ronald E. McNair Chair with the "Mount Rushmore of Female Donors"

Thanks to the contributions of three women Harris calls the "Mount Rushmore" of female donors in South Carolina—Ms. Darla Moore, Ms. Anita Zucker, and Ms. Marva Smalls—the Ronald E. McNAIR Center for Aerospace Innovation and Research was launched. The McNAIR Center houses the Zucker Institute for Aerospace Innovation and holds an endowment for scholarships. On September 30, 2013, Dr. Zafer Gürdal was installed as the Ronald E. McNair Chair and Technical Director of the McNAIR Center. We hosted a dinner that evening to honor Dr. Gürdal, Mrs. Cheryl McNair, the McNairs' son, Reginald, and the major donors to the McNAIR Center.

The reception room was filled with incredibly successful, inspirational adults who started out in life with little materially and faced obstacles that included social constructs fostering repression. The central figure of course was unfortunately absent. Ron McNair was a Ph.D. physicist who became an astronaut and planned to become a faculty member at USC had he not perished in the 1986 Challenger explosion. As a young boy, McNair was not allowed to borrow books from the public library until the police were called and, in the presence of his mother, the officer suggested the librarian let him borrow the books. He was guided toward studying music because it wasn't expected that he could pursue physics. With a strong mother, he followed his dreams and fulfilled his ambitions, proving naysayers wrong.

The benefactors of the McNAIR Center share a common commitment to excellent educational opportunity for all. Like Ron McNair, Darla Moore from Lake City, South Carolina, faced challenges and had to break down barriers in the business world, a male-dominated arena. With the inspiration of her father, who motivated her to be the best she could be, she became one of the most powerful and influential women in business—as the cover of *Fortune* magazine declared in September 1997. Today one of Darla's primary philanthropic commitments is to create the best curricula for training teachers to optimally meet the educational needs of today's students. She sees clearly that the future of South Carolina and our nation depends on the educational success of all our children.

Anita Zucker, Dr. Zafer Gürdal, Reginald McNair, Cheryl McNair, Darla Moore, and Marva Smalls at the investiture of Dr. Gürdal as the Ronald E. McNair Chair and Technical Director of the McNAIR Center.
PHOTOGRAPH BY JASON AYER.

A toast to the donors and Ron McNair. PHOTOGRAPH BY JASON AYER.

Marva Smalls, also a native of the Pee Dee region, is now executive vice president of public affairs, and chief of staff for Nickelodeon Group and executive vice president of global inclusion strategy for Viacom. Having grown up in a family that valued education highly, Marva says she benefitted from being around so many people who believed there was "no such thing as somebody else's child" and who guided and encouraged her to take advantage of opportunities for new experiences. Her donation to the McNAIR Center is for scholarships to bring rural, minority students into computer science and engineering. She is creating opportunities for "her children," students from the Pee Dee, and she knows they will be inspired by the life of Ron McNair.

Anita Zucker is the daughter of Holocaust survivors who came to America to start a new life of freedom. She is chair and CEO of the InterTech group, the second largest privately held corporation in South Carolina. It produces materials used in areas such as aerospace, aviation, and power generation. As a former schoolteacher, she values education and uses the power of her philanthropy to support all levels of education from preschool to university and to promote progressive training for teachers. She was influenced by her parents' commitment to family and community, and through her many philanthropic gifts, she hopes—as the Jewish philosophy "tikkun olam" teaches—to "repair the world."

On a personal note, I was also moved that day because my niece is a recipient of an award from the Ronald E. McNair Post-Baccalaureate Achievement Program, which was funded by the U.S. Congress after the Challenger disaster. The award was instrumental in inspiring her, a minority student, to seek her Ph.D. after graduating from Hunter College in New York City. She currently attends the University of Michigan. And now, because of the generosity and commitment of three exceptional women, we have a local tribute to Ron McNair. As Darla Moore often says, Ron McNair achieved great respect across the United States, and we need to do more to recognize him in his home state of South Carolina.

Justices Stephen Breyer and Antonin Scalia with S.C. Chief Justice Jean Toal. PHOTOGRAPH BY KEITH MCGRAW.

USC trustees Miles Loadholt and William Hubbard with former U.S. secretary of education and S.C. governor Richard Riley, USC president Harris Pastides, and former S.C. attorney general, now governor, Henry McMaster. PHOTOGRAPH BY KEITH MCGRAW.

❧ Supreme Court Justices

During our years here at USC, it has been a distinct honor and privilege to meet Supreme Court justices, presidents, vice presidents, senators, and congressmen. To meet such leaders and gain a little firsthand insight into their personalities and beliefs is a true benefit of being First Lady at USC.

U.S. Supreme Court Justices Antonin Scalia and Stephen Breyer shared the stage at the USC School of Law on January 20, 2012. Our law students and the local community of lawyers and judges were in attendance to hear them debate the meaning of the Constitution. That evening we hosted a reception for them at the President's House, where the debate ended and the jokes about political advertisements during election season wouldn't quit. As I recall, Senator Lindsey Graham introduced the topic during his remarks, and the evening continued with levity, refreshments, and lots of photo opportunities. I was tickled when Justice Scalia took the time to nibble at the buffet between photographs. There's nothing that touches the heart of a hostess like guests enjoying the food.

On another occasion we hosted Justice Sonya Sotomayor, who was given an honorary degree during the May 2011 commencement. She gave a personal and inspirational speech about the challenges and opportunities that led her to the U.S. Supreme Court. It was gratifying that, at the conclusion

Mr. and Mrs. I. S. Leevy Johnson with Justice Breyer.
PHOTOGRAPH BY KEITH MCGRAW.

Nancy and Dodie Anderson with Lou Kennedy at the Girl Scout
benefit. PHOTOGRAPH BY JASON AYER.

of the honorary-degree dinner, Justice Sotomayor shared how impressed she was with our university. Harris has a collection of some 120 baseballs signed by distinguished visitors to the university. When he asked Justice Sotomayor to sign a ball, she initially refused, but by the end of the evening she offered to sign it, saying: "If I see this on eBay I'm coming after you!"

❧ August 25, 2016: Girl Scout Benefit

Dodie Anderson and Lou and Bill Kennedy are major donors to USC athletics and academics. In 2016 they joined forces with Dodie's daughter Nancy at the President's House to launch a campaign to fund the construction of a leadership center for the Mountains to Midlands chapter of the Girl Scouts of America. Located on the Congaree River, the facility will provide opportunities for overnight lodging, outdoor adventures, and education in the STEM disciplines. It is named in the memory of Cathy Novinger, a local businesswoman and role model for girls and young woman. Dodie, Lou, and Bill led the effort with their generosity, and others were inspired by their commitment to our community. All necessary funds have been raised.

❧ Happy Times with Special Friends

We met Norman and Gerry Sue Arnold long before we became residents of the President's House. When Harris was the dean of the School of Public Health, the Arnolds made a generous gift that allowed the University of South Carolina to become one of the few schools in the country to have a named school of public health. With their support, not only did the school become known as the Arnold School of Public Health, but a new building was constructed, scholarships were endowed, and most recently a center for geriatric health was initiated.

At the time of his original gift, Norman Arnold explained that he chose to support public health because he had survived a serious cancer. Since he felt he was granted a second chance, he wanted everyone in our state and beyond to have the opportunity for good health.

Gerry Sue and Norman and Harris and I have been friends since 1999. We have shared holidays and birthdays. I'll always remember once when Norman said he wished he'd worked longer so he would have had more money to give away. In October 2016 at eighty-seven years of age, Norman passed

Janice and Bob McNair (back row center) with one class of the 2015 McNair Scholars.
PHOTOGRAPH BY JASON AYER.

away. We miss him, but his legacy will live on. He continues to inspire us to do more for others, especially to protect and promote health and wellness.

Another couple who became known to us through their generosity to the university is Bob and Janice McNair of Houston, Texas. The McNairs have supported a large endowment that allows us to bring in twenty top out-of-state students on full four-year scholarships every year. Bob was a North Carolinian who entered the University of South Carolina and became president of the student body. He credits the university for helping him prepare for the road to success and for bringing him to the home state of his lovely and evergracious wife, Janice.

Harris and I are so blessed to know Bob and Janice and consider them our dear friends. Once a year we have a dinner for them and the eighty McNair Scholars. They are so generous in giving their time to our students, who are universally thrilled to meet them and to be enveloped in their warmth.

One of my favorite memories is when our piano virtuoso, Marina Lomazov, and her talented husband, Joseph Rackers, performed for the McNair Scholars in 2010. The McNairs love music, art, and sports, so after the concert we visited with Coach and Mrs. Steve Spurrier.

The McNairs' commitment to students doesn't end with the University of South Carolina. They have endowed scholarships at Columbia College (Janice's alma mater) and many other universities and have supported programs at eight universities to help students understand the roots and impact of the American economic system.

During their visits to USC, Bob and Janice stay with us in the President's House. I look forward to catching up with them at the conclusion of the official events because they have become like family.

Gerry Sue and Norman Arnold flanked by son Ben (left) and USC Capital Campaign Chairman David Seaton (right) at the 2015 gala.
PHOTOGRAPH BY KEITH MCGRAW.

Reflections on Being First Lady

I have often considered it a good thing that Harris and I came to our positions when our children were already adults. I would have found it difficult to balance the traditional role of First Lady at USC with rearing young children. Hearing the tales of active children and animals running through the house was endearing. Still our schedule can be grueling. When our long days conclude, we often collapse—not the best with little ones. It sounds as though Mrs. Holderman worked to stay engaged with her children and to create a "normal" childhood for them. I know her efforts succeeded because her daughters are such wonderful people.

I agree with Donna and Ben Sorensen that the folks who work here in the President's House and in the Special Events Office become like family. At first this was a bit of an adjustment for me. I wasn't used to having household help every day in my private home. Yet we have developed a trust that is the foundation for our relationships—thus the "work family." I'd find it difficult to be without them now. They thoughtfully take care of so many of the logistics, so we can be more available to the university.

My relationship with this work family provides a counterpoint to the thousands of very short conversations I have with people I don't see again until the same event the following year, or perhaps never. These are interesting, intelligent people with whom I would love to develop friendships, but as First Lady, I'm already on to the next event.

Pam Bowman and her special-events staff plan and execute all the presidential events. They also help me organize book tours and speaking engagements to promote wellness and the traditional Mediterranean diet. Basically they help me coordinate whatever I do. They have creative ideas for making each endeavor memorable for participants. A member of their staff travels with me to speaking engagements and makes sure all logistics are flawless, even when they work with groups who may not be quite as well organized as they are. I really appreciate their companionship in my travels around the state and beyond. I'm usually fatigued after presentations, and it's nice not to have to get behind the wheel of a car. We also use our travel time to review and plan for upcoming events. No time is wasted!

There is no doubt that I don't bear all the stresses of the university that Harris or his executive team bear. You might justly characterize my role as being involved in all the "fun stuff without the tough stuff." Entertaining is usually not contentious, and public health and wellness are finally becoming well accepted. But in sharing stories with other SEC first spouses (we meet annually), I've explained that on our long car rides to the beach, I prefer to drive separately from Harris, who takes one call after another. They don't seem to bother him, but I can feel myself absorbing tension when I should be starting to relax. My colleagues who live similar lives to mine have gotten a good laugh at the thought of me listening to NPR or singing along with oldies while Harris, way ahead of me on the highway, is solving the many concerns of the day. A secret to survival for me is knowing what I can handle. Driving two cars at times is essential.

Even though I bear little official responsibility for the workings of the university, the heartbreaks hit me just as hard: the loss of young lives, the senseless tragedies that befall us. But living in this community has also afforded me the opportunity to witness the resilience of the human spirit and the strength that can grow from roots of faith, even in the face of devastation. I have been buoyed by our families in

The Special Events Office team: Ryan Fanning Reed, Lisa Robinette, Meagan Crowl, Pam Bowman, Betsy Suddeth, and Alysha Battaglia. PHOTOGRAPH BY KEITH MCGRAW.

crisis. Their faith and strength resonate through their pain, and I've learned from them. As I mentioned previously, this job has been an impetus for Harris and me to pray together, and we pray with a faith that has been demonstrated to us time and again by our community. The ultimate example of faith, grace, and forgiveness by the families of the Charleston Nine, who were slain at Emanuel AME Church in Charleston, compels us to grow in our faith and capacity to forgive. I was not surprised by the strength of these families for I've witnessed the same thing here at USC.

I have the best job in the world. Nobody reports to me, and I don't report to anybody. I don't have a job description, but I learned from Mrs. Norma Palms and Mrs. Donna Sorensen about hosting and perpetuating the caring "small college" feel of this major university. The culture of the University of South Carolina was what convinced us to move here twenty years ago. When Harris became president, I said it's up to us to foster and enrich that wonderful nurturing culture. I'm sure it has roots in southern hospitality.

Although I never had the pleasure of meeting Mrs. Virginia Russell, I've come to believe that through her warmth, hospitality, and respect for the students, she contributed greatly to the culture we've inherited. I loved hearing that she would introduce herself to students on the Horseshoe and offer them homemade cookies. She encouraged them to become involved in the university, to let her and her husband know about their college experience, and to offer suggestions for improvement.

Harris's role and mine both require physical and emotional stamina. We work hard to keep up a fitness regime, eat well, and get enough sleep. But our fortitude is definitely best fed by the positive energy of our community. We appreciate the vast numbers of people—students, faculty, staff, and alumni—who have taken the time to tell us, "You're doing a good job" or "Thank you for all you do for the university." Such kindnesses keep us energized, and motivate us to do more.

Living at the heart of campus means that we have the resources to be among the best-informed, best-educated, and best-entertained folks in the state and beyond. We have access to guest lecturers, distinguished professors, world leaders, symphony concerts, dance performances, theater,

A serene moment on the Horseshoe. PHOTOGRAPH BY KEITH MCGRAW.

opera, and just about every type of sporting event one can name. Most evenings there are many competing events, and we need to decide what to attend. Often Harris and I "divide and conquer," so we can be present to more members of our community and support their interests and activities.

We enjoy the vibrant life that comes with what some have called a fishbowl. The President's House is definitely not the house down the private dirt road or at the end of the quiet cul-de-sac. But I've been surprised by how calm life on the Horseshoe has been. The students have respected our privacy despite my urgings to come and ring the doorbell (before 9:00 P.M. only). We occasionally hear students who live

next door in Rutledge at about 2:00 A.M. on Sunday mornings. I listen to be sure I hear laughter and not distress before falling back to sleep.

We haven't had demonstrations on the Horseshoe like the ones Cissie Jones remembers. Nor have we had massive panty raids or any reason for the president to be called out to quiet students during the night, as Donald Russell recounted. We have groups of students who meet on the Horseshoe, play guitars, and sing. We see students in hammocks hanging in the trees, and many games of Frisbee. The Horseshoe is our collective green space, and we are happiest when it is filled with life on a sunny day.

Like Nancy Holderman and Cissie Jones, I've had what I perceived to be an encounter with a ghost in the McKissick bedroom. It was one night when I was upset with Harris because he was trying to sleep and was intolerant of my reading light. I reminded him that when he reads at night, I simply turn away, close my eyes, and sleep. That wasn't working for him, so I left the room feeling annoyed.

I went to the McKissick room, climbed into the bed, and started to read. After only a minute or two, the bedside lamp went out. I thought that was strange, but chalked it up to old wiring. I turned the light back on and in seconds it went off again. At that moment I had the distinct impression I was being told to go back to my own bed, forgive my husband, and go to sleep. I thought, all right, all right, I'm going! And I did.

In this book I've shared fond memories of times I will always cherish. There have been many more, and I know there will be even more ahead of us. A feature of my life in the President's House is that, with full days and evenings, there is little time to waste. We live in the moment. One evening off can feel like a week-long vacation. Harris and I have learned to maximize the downtime and not overbook the nights off. Several times a year, I schedule visits to see family in New York, California, and Connecticut. Fortunately they like to visit here as well. At least every few years, we try to take a family vacation with our children and grandchildren. I feel fortunate to have good friends who understand when there are long lapses between our visits. I believe I will catch up with my longtime friends during retirement.

Another important part of the tradition of USC is putting family first. That has made it so much easier when regretting my absence from important university events. I spent weeks in California after the births of our granddaughters, because those special times are irreplaceable in the life of a family. That was a lesson I learned during Mrs. Holderman's funeral, when her eldest grandchild gave the eulogy and noted the special and unique relationship Mrs. Holderman had with each of her ten grandchildren. I want mine to know me in the same way, and that requires my time, attention, and love.

Finally I believe institutions of higher learning are the jewel in the crown of America. Countries all over the world appreciate the model we have built, and many seek to emulate it. Ours is a noble mission to educate young minds to think more deeply, to seek and strive, to become leaders. I am extremely proud to be part of one of the earliest publicly funded universities in the nation. This is a university that has reinvented itself through the changing times of its history

and will continue to be a vibrant ever-changing academic community. To be one among twenty-eight families who have led a distinguished institution such as the University of South Carolina is awe inspiring. Harris and I take our responsibility to the university seriously, and we enjoy it. We have fun. I believe living in the President's House must be viewed within this context. It presents an opportunity to be a steward of tradition and an agent of change. I live here with appreciation for this opportunity and a personal commitment to engaging in efforts that are uplifting to this wonderful community.

I would love to close with one sentence that articulates all that life in the President's House has truly meant to me. Instead I've shared these musings because I realize that it may take a long time after we complete our work here to fully process and appreciate all that has happened and will happen in this home on the Horseshoe.

Sugar maple given by Katharine Erickson and Andrew Pastides on the occasion of their father's investiture as twenty-eighth president.
PHOTOGRAPH BY KEITH MCGRAW.

PART THREE

Entertainment Ideas for Your House

Floral Arrangements

We are so fortunate to have Don Staley as our presidential catering manager. Don is present at all events held at the President's House and those hosted by the president elsewhere on campus. In addition to training and supervising catering staff, he has an artistic eye for décor, selects color schemes for events, and designs and creates centerpieces for our tables. We are serious when we say that "when Don retires, we'll need at least two people to replace him." Don has distinguished himself with three significant international catering awards from Catersource, held in Las Vegas. In 2009 his tablescape won most innovative and third-place best in show. In 2010 he won most innovative, most creative, and best in show, and in 2011 he was awarded best in show.

I've included six of Don's creative ideas for floral arrangements you can make at home. A supply list and step-by-step directions accompany each photograph.

With Don Staley, the creative genius behind our tablescapes.
PHOTOGRAPH BY KEITH MCGRAW.

PHOTOGRAPH BY KEITH MCGRAW

❧ Book Arrangement

Books make a great prop at a university. Don has executed many variations on a theme using faux books for the vessels of floral arrangements.

SUPPLIES

3×4×3-inch floral foam

1 small green-plastic economy bowl (found at floral-supply or craft stores) or a 6-inch plate

1 faux book (found at craft stores)

5 roses

5 miniature calla lilies

5 wooden floral picks

3 gerbera daisies

Assorted greenery (cut from the garden)

3 tulips

5 solidago

PROCEDURE

Soak the block of floral foam for 10 minutes, until bubbles stop rising.

Place the foam in the economy bowl or use a small 6-inch plate as your base.

Place the bowl with floral foam into the base of the hollow book.

Cut the roses into various lengths depending on the size of the book. Angle the roses as you place them into the foam.

Because calla stems are soft, add a floral pick to each one. Add the calla lilies in positions that look good to you.

Add the gerbera daisies near the center of the arrangement.

Add pieces of greenery cut to approximately 3 inches in length.

Add the 3 tulips and the solidago as the last step.

This book container would also be great as a gift box or to hold a dozen cookies. It could also hold silverware for a buffet or be used to display fresh vegetables.

PHOTOGRAPH BY KEITH MCGRAW

PHOTOGRAPH BY KEITH MCGRAW

❧ Carrot and Tulip Arrangement

Here's a lovely, sustainable arrangement that might come right from your yard. Pull a bunch of carrots, tops and all, from your vegetable garden. (If you are faithful Gamecocks like us, you will be happy to grow atomic red carrots!) Add a bouquet of tulips or daffodils cut from your yard, and you'll have a charming arrangement for your table.

SUPPLIES

10–12 assorted carrots with the tops intact

6–8-inch vase

Cool tap water

10–12 tulips

PROCEDURE

Wash the carrots and put them in your vase. Then fill it with water.

Cut the tulips to your desired height. They will continue to grow 1 or 2 more inches during the life of the arrangement. Place the tulips in the vase so that the carrots line the vase and the tulips are all within the circle of carrots.

❧ Football Helmet

Football tailgates may not always deserve roses, but on ESPN GameDay, Don pulls out all the stops. Here's a mighty Gamecock centerpiece that shouts "Victory!"

SUPPLIES

3×4×9-inch floral foam

Helmet chip and dip set

12–18 roses

Greenery

1 bunch of daisies

PROCEDURE

Soak the foam for 10 minutes, until the bubbles stop rising.

Place the foam in the chip container.

Cut off the foam, leaving ½ inch above the rim of the container. Use the leftover foam to wedge in the main foam piece.

Place your tallest rose (up to 18 inches long) in the center of the foam. Add 5 to 7 roses around the base, and then add 4 more roses midway between the top rose and lower roses. Continue to add roses (up to 18 total).

Add your choice of greenery. We usually use pittosporum from our garden. Fill in with as many white daisies as needed, cutting their stems various lengths to give visual depth.

Finish the arrangement by placing cut pieces of pittosporum in the helmet-guard area (where the dip is meant to go) to fill in and hide the foam.

PHOTOGRAPH BY KEITH MCGRAW

❧ Green Present

A present arrangement to use on a Christmas table, this one can easily be converted to a centerpiece for a birthday or any other occasion. The green present lasts a long time.

SUPPLIES

12×9×6-inch floral foam

12–15 bunches of green button mums

Plastic wrap

18×24-inch silver tray

White ribbon and bow

Stems of holly with berries

Holiday greenery

PROCEDURE

Soak the foam in water for 30 minutes, until all bubbles stop rising.

While the foam is soaking, cut the green button mums ¼ inch to ½ inch in length.

Cover the surface of the tray with plastic wrap. The tray should be large enough to allow at least 2 inches of clearance on each side of the foam you are using.

Place the wet block of foam on the plastic wrap.

Insert mums in a single row all around the bottom edge of the foam. Offset the next row and continue all around the foam. Follow the same procedure until the foam is completely covered in mums.

Top the arrangement with stems of holly and holiday greenery and add a pretty bow. Place additional holiday greenery around the base.

If you remove the ribbon and mist the arrangement every few days, you can prolong this arrangement's life for 10–14 days.

PHOTOGRAPH BY KEITH MCGRAW

⚜ Skillet Arrangement

With my interest in sustainability and organic gardening, we have found many occasions to create whimsical food-centered arrangements. This one, made in a cast-iron skillet is especially fun.

SUPPLIES

3×4×7-inch floral foam

8–10-inch cast-iron skillet

8 roses

3 artichokes

3 wooden floral picks

Assorted greenery

2 stems of green button mums

2–3 heads of garlic

Knife and fork

PROCEDURE

Soak floral foam for 10 minutes, until bubbles stop rising.

Place the floral foam in the skillet. You don't need to tape or glue it because the foam is usually heavy enough to stay in place.

Cut the stems of four roses to about 2 or 3 inches and insert the roses in the foam near the rim of the skillet. Cut the stem of one rose to about 5 inches and place it at the center of the arrangement.

Place 3 more roses between the top rose and the base roses.

Place picks in the artichoke stems and insert them into the arrangement.

Insert greenery (such as pittosporum, which holds up for a long time) as you like.

Fill in empty spaces with a few green button mums.

Insert the heads of garlic without using picks (which would cause an odor).

Insert the knife and fork.

❧ White Arrangement

There is nothing that says elegance more than an all-white arrangement. Choose the flowers you like best and add some greenery from your shrubs for a classic look that is perfect for summer.

SUPPLIES

10–12-inch vase

Cool tap water

1 packet floral food

Assorted greenery

5 white hydrangeas (cut at 12–14 inches)

5–7 white peonies (cut at 14–16 inches)

White ranunculi (optional)

Green hydrangea (optional)

White roses (optional)

PROCEDURE

Fill your vase with cool water and add the packet of floral food.

Add several stems of greenery cut from your garden, forming a collar and framework in the vase.

Add the hydrangeas so that the blooms float above the rim of the vase.

Add the peonies between the hydrangea blooms.

Ranunculi are a nice addition to this arrangement. You might also add several green hydrangea blooms, a white rose or two, or any springtime flowers.

May or June is the best time for purchasing peonies.

President's House Menus

The first and probably most exciting charge for me as First Lady was to assist in the selection process for hiring an executive chef for presidential catering. He or she was to be an employee of the university food-service provider, but his or her primary responsibility would be to plan and execute the menus for presidential events. Since I would work on menu planning with the chef, I was invited to participate in the process. Through preliminary interviews, the field was narrowed to the three best candidates. I reviewed their resumes, which all looked good. I had two major concerns; the first was how well they could cook. The second was how well they could cook creative, plant-based, ethnic, local, sustainable, and—very important to me—*healthful* and delicious meals. Determined to have each of the three finalists cook for us, the general manager and I discussed how best to test their cooking prowess. I suggested creating a market basket of ingredients and giving them a time period within which to create a four-course meal. I enjoyed the element of catching them off-guard, as in a Food Network challenge, but I also knew that without such a test, each chef would simply prepare personal specialties, which wouldn't necessarily address my concerns.

I selected the same ingredients for all three candidates: They were sea bass, lamb chops, arugula, beets, kale, berries, pecans, goat cheese, quinoa, and cardamom. The plan was to give each chef four hours and a kitchen and see what they would come up with. I can remember saying that, if anyone made a surf-and-turf entrée by putting the fish and the lamb together, I wouldn't vote for them.

I knew we had created a reasonable challenge when one of the finalists dropped out. The second one participated, but

his creativity was lacking, and he fell into the trap of using the two proteins in the same course, which left us with our first chef, James Ellison. His preparation was by far and away the best—creative, delicious, and beautiful on the plate. I chuckled when Harris, who was up to his eyeballs in his own job and hadn't paid much attention to the process, praised James, saying: "It's uncanny how you happened to prepare all the things Patricia loves!"

Since 2008 we have held the presidential chef recruitment three additional times. It seems two to three years is about the job span of a chef at an institution like ours. The events are often clustered around big games and holidays, sometimes more than one for every day of the month. Guest counts can be four to six hundred. Chefs like ours don't have regular hours, and the demands vary widely. Our current chef is Peter Zoellinger, who previously cooked on a cruise ship and married the ship's singer, who is from the South. We are fortunate that Peter was looking for a position in this region when we had an executive chef opening.

One question I get asked often is whether the chef hired for presidential catering cooks for us all the time. The answer is yes and no. He cooks for all the events Harris and I host on campus, which during the heart of the school year are nearly nightly. I work closely with the chef to select the menus for these events, most of which are stand-up receptions where heavy hors d'oeuvres are served. We rarely eat anything in the presence of our guests, but samples of the repast are sent to our kitchen. We typically eat at 8:30 or 9:00 P.M., after everyone has gone home, in front of our television, with a glass of wine—with our feet propped up and without conversing.

On the evenings when we don't have events, I cook. If it's a weekend we cook together. Harris and I have always enjoyed

Blake Clevenger, presidential chef (2014–2016), and I testing recipes. PHOTOGRAPH BY KEITH MCGRAW.

our meals, from preparation to dessert. We cook simply, consume few processed foods, and take care with the presentation of the meal. Just before we sit down to eat, Harris takes a quick picture of the table and texts it to our children (in California and New York) with the one word heading, "NOW." I suppose this act is a not-so-veiled attempt to make them want to come home! We *do* converse during these meals.

So what are we having for presidential events? I like to offer a variety of tasty and healthful foods that are different from the usual fare. When I became First Lady, I heard that the trustees feared I would take away their fried chicken and hot dogs at football games. I'm sure others thought I might promote only healthy options regardless of flavor. Every once

in a while someone will try to hide what they are eating from me. These folks apparently see me as the food police.

My passion is to promote the traditional Mediterranean diet, but we do not limit ourselves to that for university events. We offer a variety of ethnic foods, including lots of vegetable dishes, and when meats are served, they are grass fed. We rarely prepare anything deep fried and offer no processed foods. We provide selections that accommodate the desires of vegetarians and vegans as well as omnivores. Based on the responses of our guests, I think we have been successful in keeping everyone happy, at least most of the time. The following are sample menus from some of our events.

Fresh Mango and Avocado Frisée Salad
with Feta and Orange-Dijon Vinaigrette

Rosemary Grilled Salmon
over Summer Corn and Edamame
Succotash, with Kale Salad

Raspberry Buckle
with Vanilla-Bean Ice Cream

September Donor Luncheon for 6

Heirloom Lettuces
with Cara Cara Orange, Daikon Radish,
Pecans, Feta, and Citrus Vinaigrette

Sundried-Tomato Pesto Quinoa Salad

Crispy Avocado Tacos with Salsa Verde

Carved Chimichurri Grilled
Grass-Fed Flank Steak

Shrimp Sliders

Apple Toffee Spring Rolls

Winter Student Scholars Reception for 20

Hearts of Palm
with Micro Mesclun, Caramelized Onion,
and Citrus Vinaigrette

Pan Seared Mahimahi Topped
with Shrimp Bobo
(*Vegetarian Option:* Coconut-Crusted
Portobello Mushroom)

Citrus Jasmine Rice and Roasted Okra

Sweet Corn Brûlée

Winter Donor Society Luncheon for 184

Peach and Brie in Puff Pastry

Roasted Vegetable Crostini

Heirloom Lettuces
with Hearts of Palm, Avocado,
Blood Orange, Toasted Pumpkin Seeds,
and Citrus Avocado Vinaigrette

Grilled Tamarind Basil-Glazed Poulet Rouge

Southeastern Family Farms
Carved Grass-Fed Strip Steak
with Sweet Onion Fig Sauce and
Assorted Multigrain Rolls

Roasted Vegetable Gougères

Ricotta Tarts with Dried-Fruit Compote

Winter Faculty Authors Reception for 80

International Stations

French

Chopped Salad Niçoise

Rosemary Lamb Meatballs
with Apricot Crème Fraîche

Wild Mushroom Vol-au-Vents

African

Spiced Red-Lentil Dip
with Whole Wheat Pitas and Garden Crudités

Tandoori Shrimp
with Cilantro Yogurt Sauce

Sweet and Nutty Moroccan Couscous

Asian

Asian Slaw Salad

Vegetable Egg Roll

Steamed Chicken Dumplings

Dessert Station

Macaroons

Mini Éclairs

Melktarts (Milk Tarts)

Chinese Five-Spice Mini Carrot Cupcakes
with Ginger Cream-Cheese Frosting

Autumn International Students Reception for 375

Garlic Hummus

Muhammara Dip
(Roasted Red Pepper and Walnut)
with Gourmet Garden Crudités,
Grilled Crostini

Chopped Tender Kale and Quinoa Salad
with Red Grapes, Sweet Red Pepper,
Sunflower Seeds, and Parmesan Cheese
in Meyer Lemon Vinaigrette

Grilled Jerk Chicken Bites
with Banana Mango Coulis

Shredded Moroccan Lamb
atop Pita with Tzatziki Sauce,
Lemon Zest, and Mint

Adobo Roasted Shrimp

Lemon Bar Bites

Melon Ball Salad with Mint

Parents Weekend Reception for 650

Lemon Garlic Hummus

Roasted Red Pepper and Feta Dip

Toasted Pita Points

Garden Crudités

Antipasto Display
Feta Wedges, Assorted Olives,
Stuffed Grape Leaves, Roasted Red Peppers,
Asparagus, Cherry Tomatoes

Greek Bruschetta

Cabbage, Walnut, and Cranberry Salad
with Balsamic Vinaigrette

Tabbouleh
with Herbs, Dried Fruit, and Nuts

Petite Grilled Chicken Gyros
with Cucumber Salsa and Tzatziki Sauce

Lamb Moussaka

Red-Pepper Flake Shrimp

Sautéed Greens
with Garlic and Extra Virgin Olive Oil

Greek Yogurt
with Strawberries, Poached Figs, and Honey

Baklava Tartlets

Milopita
(Greek Apple and Walnut Pie)

OPA! All Faculty Party for 500
(Inspired by *Greek Revival: Cooking for Life*)

Tea Sandwiches

Roast Turkey
with Cranberry Cream on Honey Wheat

Herb Braised Crimini Mushroom
and Havarti on Rye

Brisket of Beef
with Horseradish Cream on Sourdough

Cookie Selection

Chocolate Peppermint

Shortbread

Sugar Cookies
with Red and Green Sanding Sugar

Sugar-Free Cookies

Beverages

Hot Spiced Apple Cider

Pomegranate Iced Tea

Citrus Water

Holiday Faculty and Staff Open House for 700

President's House Recipes

This chapter begins with three recipes served in earlier administrations: the Country Captain chicken and Strawberry Shortcake that Virginia Russell served at Senior Dinners and the Italian Cream Cake that Rick Gant baked for Donna Sorensen's birthdays. These are followed by ten recipes served at President's House events under the direction of Chef Blake Clevenger.

❧ Virginia Russell's Country Captain

(Adapted from Cecily Brownstone)

As a small tribute to Mrs. Virginia Russell, the original First Lady of the modern President's House, I prepared Country Captain, as I believe she did from an early Joy of Cooking *recipe. It is, for a modest investment of time, a savory dish, which received positive reviews from my taste testers, the cast and crew of the President's House.*

¼ cup flour

1 teaspoon salt

¼ teaspoon freshly
     ground black pepper

1 broiler chicken, about
     3½ pounds, cut into 12 pieces

¼ cup butter

1 medium-size onion, diced large

1 medium-size green bell pepper,
     diced large

1 clove garlic, peeled and crushed

3–4 large tomatoes (blanched,
     skin removed, and juice reserved),
     chopped

1½ teaspoons curry powder

½ teaspoon dried thyme

3 tablespoons currants

⅓ cup blanched almonds for garnish

Preheat the oven to 350 degrees.

Combine the flour, salt, and pepper in a large bowl with a fork or whisk.

Dredge the chicken pieces in the flour mixture to coat on all sides.

Melt the butter in a large Dutch oven on the stovetop over medium heat. (My favorite Dutch oven is Le Creuset.) Place half the chicken pieces in the Dutch oven and cook until they are evenly browned on all sides. Set them on waxed paper. Brown the remaining chicken pieces in the same way and remove them to the waxed paper.

Reduce the temperature to low. Add the chopped onion, diced pepper, and crushed garlic to the pot and stir to loosen the browned bits from the bottom. Add the chopped tomatoes and reserved juice, curry powder, and dried thyme. Heat thoroughly, stirring to combine all ingredients.

Add the chicken pieces and stir gently to combine.

Bake uncovered in the oven for 25 minutes, then add the currants and bake five minutes longer.

Serve over steamed Carolina Gold rice and top with almonds.

Serves 6

❧ Strawberry Shortcake Mrs. Russell's Way

I fear my attempt to re-create Mrs. Russell's strawberry shortcake may not taste like mother's to Donald, but I hope you will enjoy it.

STRAWBERRY LAYER

2 quarts ripe strawberries

4 teaspoons sugar

Process 1 quart of ripe strawberries with 2 teaspoons of sugar in a food processor. Set aside.

Holding back 2–3 strawberries for garnish, slice the second quart of strawberries and place them in a bowl with 2 teaspoons of sugar. Set aside.

SHORTCAKE

The following biscuit recipe is a dessert version of one found in Nathalie Dupree and Cynthia Graubart's *Mastering the Art of Southern Cooking*. For a northern girl lacking biscuit experience, this recipe proved fool proof and earned me a marriage proposal.

2½ cups self-rising flour

1¼ cups heavy cream

1 tablespoon sugar

Melted butter for brushing

Preheat the oven to 450 degrees.

Brush a 9-inch round cake pan with melted butter.

Whisk 2 cups of flour in a large bowl.

Use the back of your hand to make a well in the center of the flour.

Pour the cream into the well slowly and, using your hand, blend the flour into the cream until it is incorporated. Sprinkle the sugar over the flour and cream mixture and blend it in gently with your hands. Be careful not to over-work the dough, or you'll risk tough biscuits.

(CONTINUED)

Turn the dough onto a floured surface and with floured hands press it into a ball.

Gently press the ball into a circle 1-inch thick. Then use a 2-inch biscuit cutter to cut it into 8 rounds. Brush any excess flour off the biscuits. Place them in the pan with their sides touching and bake them on the top shelf of the oven for 10–14 minutes until light golden brown. After 6 minutes, rotate the pan in the oven so the back is now the front. Check the biscuit bottoms to see if they are darkening too fast. If so, place a cookie sheet directly below them on a lower rack. Continue baking for 4–8 minutes until the biscuits are golden brown.

Remove the biscuits from the oven and brush the tops lightly with melted butter. Let them cool turned out of the pan and upside down on a plate.

When the biscuits are cooled turn them right-side up and, using a fork, pierce each biscuit all around its middle until you can split it in half. Place each biscuit bottom on an individual dessert plate. Spoon a swirl of pureed strawberries on each biscuit bottom. Then combine the sliced berries with the remaining puree and lavish it over the biscuit bottoms.

WHIPPED CREAM TOPPING

1 cup heavy whipping cream

2 tablespoons confectionary sugar

1 teaspoon real vanilla extract

Whip the cream on high speed until it begins to thicken, then add the confectionary sugar and vanilla extract. Continue whipping until the cream is thick and fluffy.

Arrange each biscuit top to rest against its bottom artistically, then top the strawberries with a large dollop of freshly whipped cream. Garnish the cream with a small piece of ripe red strawberry and serve immediately (if not sooner).

Serves 8

Italian cream cake. PHOTOGRAPH BY KEITH MCGRAW.

❧ Italian Cream Cake

(Donna Sorensen's Birthday Cake)

If you would prefer a less sweet version of this nutty cake, I would recommend cutting the frosting recipe in half and frosting the two layers without splitting them.

CAKE

½ cup shortening at room temperature

½ cup butter at room temperature

1⅔ cups sugar

6 eggs, separated

⅜ teaspoon baking soda

½ teaspoon salt

2 cups flour

1 cup buttermilk

1 teaspoon vanilla extract

2 cups shredded coconut

1 cup chopped pecans (lightly toasted)

¼ teaspoon cream of tartar

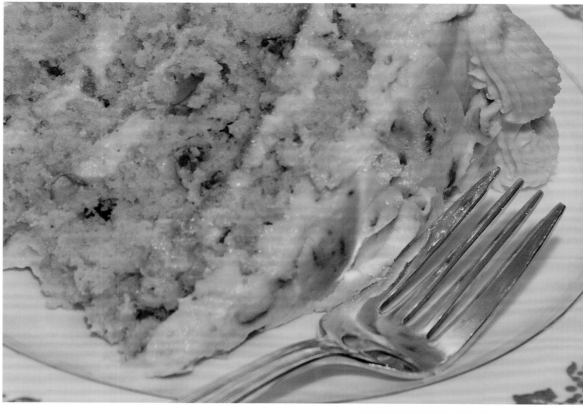

PHOTOGRAPH BY KEITH MCGRAW

Preheat the oven to 350 degrees.

Cream the shortening, butter, and sugar until light and fluffy.

Add the egg yolks one at a time and beat well after each addition.

In a separate mixing bowl, combine the baking soda, salt, and flour.

Add some flour mixture to the creamed mixture alternating with some buttermilk. Begin and end with the dry ingredients.

Stir in the vanilla, coconut, and pecans.

Beat the egg whites with the cream of tartar until stiff peaks form.

Fold the egg white mixture into the cake batter.

Grease and flour two 10-inch round cake pans. Divide the batter equally between the two pans.

Bake the layers in the center of the oven for 30–40 minutes, until a cake tester comes out dry.

Cool the cakes for 10 minutes on a wire rack and then remove the cakes from the pans.

Once the cakes are thoroughly cooled, split each layer in half, creating four layers.

FROSTING

1 cup butter at room temperature

16 ounces cream cheese at room temperature

8 cups confectionary sugar

1½ teaspoons vanilla extract

2 cups chopped pecans, lightly toasted

Cream the butter and cream cheese.

Gradually add the powdered sugar and vanilla extract and beat until smooth and creamy.

Set aside 1 cup of frosting for adding decorations to the frosted cake. Then add the pecans to the remaining frosting.

ASSEMBLING THE CAKE

Spread frosting between each of the layers, stacking them as you go. Frost the sides and then the top of the cake, making sure the cake is level. Decorate as desired.

Serves 16 generously

I thought it might be fun to include some recipes here that can be prepared ahead of a party. Chef Blake Clevenger offered the following, which he made for events here and at his current position at the other, far younger USC.

PHOTOGRAPH BY KEITH MCGRAW

❧ Herb-Crusted Roast Lamb Chops

Blake loves lamb in any shape or form. He typically used chops for receptions at the President's House because they are small, and the bone is a perfect "handle" for diners who are eating while standing up. Lamb and fresh herbs are a natural match.

3 lamb racks, about 24 individual chops

Sea salt

Pepper

2 tablespoons fresh thyme leaves stripped from their stems

2 tablespoons rosemary, chopped small

2 tablespoons fresh basil, chopped small

2 tablespoons parsley, chopped small

1 tablespoon minced garlic

Extra-virgin olive oil as needed

2 tablespoons Dijon mustard

2 tablespoons honey

1 tablespoon water

Preheat the oven to 400 degrees.

Cut between the bones of each rack to separate individual chops, and sprinkle salt and pepper over each lamb chop.

Rub the thyme leaves between your fingers to bring out the oils. Mix all the fresh herbs and garlic together in a bowl; stir in a little olive oil to moisten them, and set the bowl aside.

In another bowl mix together the mustard, honey, and water.

Using the bone as a handle, dip each lamb chop in the mustard mixture and then dredge it in the herb mixture, making sure to coat the chop evenly. Repeat until all the chops are coated.

Spread the chops on sheet pans. Don't try to put too many chops on a single pan. Cook them for approximately 5–8 minutes. (Some chops will be thinner and require less time.) Use a meat thermometer to probe the middle of each chop. The ideal temperature will be between 142 and 150 degrees.

Serves 16–20

❧ Naan Bread Pizza with Feta Basil Lemon and Tomatoes

When Blake worked at a luxury resort in Curaçao, Dutch West Indies, there was an Indian restaurant on site with a hand-made clay tandoor oven, which used imported white oak that burned incredibly hot at 900 degrees. The high temperature creates a delicious crust. Indian naan bread is made from a simple dough that is rolled out and stuck to the wall of the tandoor by hand. It cooks in about 1 minute. Blake used leftover naan bread to make these little pizzas for the afternoon bar menu. They are light, simple, and delicious. You can find ready-made naan bread at Indian markets or at many grocery stores, but it's best when you make it yourself.

NAAN

2¼ cups flour

1 tablespoon sugar

2 teaspoons of active dry yeast

1 teaspoon salt

½ cup, plus 4 teaspoons of room-temperature butter, separated

1 cup warm water (not over 105 degrees)

Place the flour, sugar, yeast, salt, and ½ cup butter in a mixing bowl. Mix these ingredients together with your fingers until everything is incorporated. Make a well in the center of this mixture and pour in the warm water. Mix these ingredients with your fingers for several minutes until all come together to form a ball. Finish rolling the dough into a ball by pulling and tucking under the outsides. Place the dough in a bowl that has been rubbed with 2 teaspoons butter and spread a kitchen towel over the top. Put the bowl in a warm area and let it sit for about 1 hour.

Remove the dough and cut it in half. Then cut each of these pieces in half and repeat until you have 8 pieces.

Let the pieces relax for about 10 minutes.

Flour your work surface and roll each dough piece about ¼ inch thick and 10–12 inches in diameter. Don't worry about creating perfect circles.

(CONTINUED)

The more rustic the naan looks, the better.

Heat a cast-iron skillet over medium-high heat, and add 2 teaspoons of butter. Place one dough disk in the skillet, and cook it about 1 minute or until the edges puff. Adjust the heat if necessary. Then flip the dough and cook it about 1 minute on the second side. Place the browned naan bread on a plate covered with a square of parchment paper, place another piece of parchment on the bread, and repeat until you have cooked and stacked all 8 naan breads. Set aside 4 pieces of naan for the pizza recipe. Wrap the remainder tightly in plastic. You can store it in the freezer for up to 3 months.

PIZZA

4 naan breads

8 tablespoons extra-virgin olive oil

Sea salt and freshly ground black pepper to taste

2 pints summer cherry tomatoes, cut in half

Zest of half a lemon

½ cup basil chiffonade (basil leaves stacked on top of each other, rolled up, and sliced into thin ribbons)

2 cups crumbled feta cheese

¼ cup grated Parmesan cheese

¼ teaspoon red-pepper flakes (optional)

Preheat the oven to 400 degrees.

Place each naan bread on a piece of parchment paper. Use your hands to spread extra-virgin olive oil all the way to the edge of each bread. Sprinkle with sea salt and freshly ground black pepper. Add the tomatoes, lemon zest, and basil. Sprinkle with feta cheese and then Parmesan cheese. Sprinkle with red-pepper flakes if desired. Make sure the ingredients cover the entire naan bread.

Place the pizzas on the middle rack of the oven, holding onto the parchment as you slide each pizza off.

Bake for about 8 minutes. Keep a close eye on the pizzas because every oven is different.

Using a pair of tongs, grab the edge of each pizza and slide it onto a sheet pan. Let the pizzas cool for a couple of minutes. Then slide them onto a cutting board. Cut each down the middle lengthwise and make three cuts across for 32 pieces total.

Serves 16

PHOTOGRAPH BY KEITH MCGRAW

❧ Roasted Brussels Sprouts Salad with Red Quinoa and Cranberries

4½ pounds brussels sprouts

3 tablespoons extra-virgin olive oil

3 cups red quinoa

5 cups water

Pinch of salt

DRESSING

6 cloves garlic, minced

7½ tablespoons red-wine vinegar

6 tablespoons lemon juice (from 2–3 lemons)

6 teaspoons Dijon mustard

3 teaspoons extra-virgin olive oil

¾ cup toasted slivered almonds

¾ cup dried cranberries

½ cup chopped parsley

Salt and pepper to taste

Brussels sprouts are having a resurgence. They are hearty and versatile. Blake used them in this seasonal salad, which ended up being one of the most popular dishes on the President's House menu. The addition of red quinoa, a plant protein, makes this salad an amazing vegetarian dish, but even die-hard carnivores enjoy it.

Preheat the oven to 400 degrees.

Pick through the brussels sprouts and pull off any leaves that look old or battered. Cut the sprouts into quarters or halves, depending on their size. Toss them in 3 tablespoons extra-virgin olive oil. Spread them on a sheet pan and roast them for about 20 minutes until they are caramelized but not burned.

While the brussels sprouts are roasting, rinse the quinoa, so it does not become bitter when you cook it. Place the quinoa in a medium pot with 5 cups of salted water and bring the mixture to a boil, then turn it down to a simmer, cover the pot, and cook the quinoa about 15 minutes, until most of the water is absorbed and the quinoa is tender.

When the sprouts are done, place them in a bowl with the cooked and cooled quinoa. Mix the dressing ingredients together. Pour the dressing over the brussels sprouts and quinoa, stirring until everything is well coated. Stir in the almonds, cranberries, and parsley. Stir again and add salt and pepper to taste.

Serves 16–20

❧ Seared Halibut with Thai-Style Coconut-Curry Sauce

According to Chef Blake, many people identify Thai flavors as predominant in Southeast Asia, but in reality Thai cuisine has influences from Cambodian, Laotian, and Vietnamese traditions. Originally this dish was a variation of vegetarian "boat noodles," coconut-curry sauce served with rice noodles and vegetables. Once while Blake was searing some halibut for another dish, one of his sous chefs, who was from Southeast Asia, saw Blake looking at the noodles and then the fish. They instantly had the same idea that using the noodle sauce with the fish would make a fantastic dish. That was the birth of Seared Halibut with Thai-Style Coconut-Curry Sauce.

Thai red-curry paste is available in most grocery stores. The fish monger in a store will usually cut the fish for you if you ask.

1 cup whole shallots, peeled

½ cup whole ginger, peeled

½ cup garlic cloves

4 tablespoons extra-virgin olive oil or virgin coconut oil

2 stalks lemongrass, smashed with the back of a knife and cut into 2-inch pieces

1½ tablespoons curry powder

1 tablespoon ground coriander

3 14-ounce cans coconut milk

4 tablespoons honey

4 tablespoons Thai red-curry paste

Juice of 1 freshly squeezed lime

¼ cup minced fresh cilantro

¼ cup minced fresh basil

Salt and pepper

4 pounds halibut, cut into approximately 20 3-ounce pieces

Lime wedges for garnish

Fresh cilantro and basil leaves for garnish

Preheat the oven to 300 degrees.

Chop the shallots, ginger, and garlic into small pieces. Heat a large sauce pot on medium to medium-high heat. Add 2 tablespoons of the oil, then sauté the shallots, ginger, and garlic until they are tender, about 3 minutes. They will cook quickly, so be careful not to let them burn. Add the lemongrass, curry powder, and coriander, and cook for another minute. Add the coconut milk, honey, red-curry paste, and lime juice. Bring the mixture to a boil and reduce heat to a simmer. Cook for approximately 30 minutes. Add the minced fresh cilantro and basil, and salt and pepper to taste. Discard the lemongrass. Set sauce aside.

Place a 10–12″ nonstick skillet over a high flame. Liberally salt and pepper the halibut pieces. Add 2 tablespoons of the oil to the skillet. When the oil is heated, add the halibut slowly, being careful not to splatter the hot oil. Sear each side until golden, using a spatula to turn the halibut. Then place the skillet in a 300 degree oven for approximately 3 minutes. Pour half the curry sauce over the halibut and put it back in the oven for another 3 minutes.

Serve the halibut over steamed jasmine rice or by itself on a platter. Pour the remainder of the curry sauce over the halibut. Garnish with lime wedges, fresh cilantro, and fresh basil.

Serves 16–20

❧ Shaved Fennel Salad with Red Onion, Grapefruit, Avocado, and Blue Cheese

Also called finocchio, fennel is delicious braised, caramelized, and paired with avocados. Blake created a salad in which avocado and blue cheese work together to add a rich element, while the grapefruit and fennel brighten and cut through the richness.

6 large fennel bulbs

1 large bowl of ice water

1 large red onion

1 medium bowl of ice water

6 pink grapefruit

3 Hass avocados (ripe, but a little firm)

DRESSING

2 tablespoons Dijon mustard

4½ tablespoons raspberry vinegar

3 tablespoons extra-virgin olive oil

4½ teaspoons walnut oil

Sea salt and freshly ground black
    pepper to taste

6 ounces good blue cheese, crumbled

½ cup walnut halves

PHOTOGRAPH BY KEITH MCGRAW

Cut the fronds off the fennel bulb and compost them. With a knife or a mandolin shave thin slices from across the bottom of the fennel bulb. Place the shaved fennel in the large ice-water bath. Then shave thin slices of onion and place them in the medium-sized bowl of ice water.

Drain the fennel and the onion and place them in a large bowl.

Cut off the ends of the grapefruits. Stand them up and cut the peel and pith off from the top to the bottom, following the curve of the fruit. Hold the grapefruit over the bowl with the fennel and cut the sections, just inside of the membranes. This is known as "supreming" the grapefruits. The resulting sections have no pith and no membranes. After supreming the grapefruit, squeeze the membrane over the bowl to release the juice left in it. Set the supremes aside.

Cut each avocado in half lengthwise until you hit the pit. Then twist one half of the avocado in one direction and the other half in the opposite direction until it opens and one side is left with the pit. Place the half with the pit on a cutting board, pit side up. Swing a knife blade into the middle of the seed. Hold the avocado and carefully twist the knife. The pit should come out. Run a spoon between the skin and the pulp, scooping out the pulp. Dice the pulp into ½-inch cubes and place them in the bowl with the fennel and onion slices.

Whisk together the mustard and vinegar in a small bowl, then whisk in the olive oil and walnut oil. Add the sea salt and freshly ground black pepper to taste.

Lightly fold the vinaigrette into the fennel mixture, being careful not to mash the avocado. Place the dressed salad in a serving bowl. Garnish it with blue cheese, walnuts, and the reserved grapefruit supremes.

Since the flavors are delicate, this recipe benefits from being served soon after it is made.

Serves 16–20

When Blake builds seasonal menus, he tries to find a signature recipe that defines each season. This soup captures the essence of summer without a doubt! It's light, refreshing, and colorful. You can find crème fraîche in specialty markets, or you can substitute plain Greek-style yogurt.

❧ Summer Chilled Stone-Fruit Soup with Crème Fraîche

1 medium-sized bowl
   of ice water

12 peaches

12 apricots

12 nectarines

1 lemon

2 teaspoons ground cinnamon

1 teaspoon ground ginger

1 tablespoon vanilla-bean paste

1 tablespoon honey

1 cup heavy cream

4 tablespoons crème fraîche

20 small mint leaves for garnish

Make an ice bath in a medium bowl with 4 cups of ice and 2 cups of water. Bring 2 quarts of water to a boil in a medium-sized pot. Drop fruit, one at a time, in the boiling water, leave it for about 15 seconds, then remove it to the ice bath to shock and cool it for 15 seconds. Don't leave the fruit sitting in the ice water any longer than that.

Using a paring knife, gently remove the skin from the peaches and nectarines, but leave the skin on the apricots. Cut the fruit into chunks, discarding the stems and pits.

Place the fruit in a food processor. Squeeze the lemon over the fruit to preserve its color.

Add the spices, vanilla, and honey.

Blend the mixture thoroughly. Add the cream and purée until smooth.

Place the soup in individual cups and garnish with piped crème fraîche and fresh mint.

Serves 16–20

❧ Tuscan Kale Salad with Dried Cherries, Charred Onions, Walnuts, and Poppy-Seed Vinaigrette

Kale, our new national vegetable, is heavier and heartier than other greens. It can be sautéed, steamed, and braised. This salad says fall, but it can be enjoyed year round.

DRESSING

½ cup sugar

¾ cup vinegar

2 teaspoons salt

2 teaspoons dry ground mustard

2 teaspoons grated onion

1½ cups extra virgin olive oil

2 tablespoons poppy seeds

SALAD

1 large red onion, sliced into rings

8 cups Tuscan kale with stems removed and leaves torn into small pieces

1 cup dried tart cherries

1 cup walnut halves

Salt and pepper to taste

PHOTOGRAPH BY KEITH MCGRAW

DRESSING

In a blender combine sugar, vinegar, salt, mustard, and onion. Process for 20 seconds, gradually adding oil in a slow stream. Stir in the poppy seeds.

SALAD

Grill or broil the rings of red onion until they are a little charred, not burned.

Place the Tuscan kale in a bowl and add enough dressing to coat it. Let it sit for 10 minutes. Add the rest of the ingredients—reserving some of the cherries, onion, and walnuts for garnish—and toss well. Place the salad in a serving bowl, salt and pepper to taste, and top it with the reserved garnish.

Serves 20

Everyone identifies the Fourth of July with watermelon. It is the quintessential summer fruit. This refreshing salad has the sweet, spicy, salty, and sour elements that make your tongue tingle.

❧ Watermelon Salad with Sweet Onion, Mint, Red-Chili Flakes, Feta, and Lime Syrup

4 pounds seedless watermelon, medium diced

1 large sweet Vidalia onion, shaved

Sea salt to taste

¼ cup mint leaves, chiffonade

1 tablespoon red chili flakes

1 cup crumbled feta cheese

4 tablespoons lime syrup (recipe below)

Cut the ends off the watermelon and stand it up; follow the curves of the watermelon from top to bottom to cut off the rind, which is about an inch thick.

Slice the watermelon into large disks, then cut them into a medium dice. Place the watermelon cubes into a large bowl.

With a knife or a mandolin thinly shave the sweet onion. Lightly salt the onion to soften it and add it to the watermelon.

Chiffonade the mint by stacking the leaves on top of each other, rolling up the stack, and slicing it, creating thin ribbons. Add the mint to the watermelon salad.

Sprinkle in the red chili flakes. You may use less or more than a tablespoon, depending on how spicy you like it.

Add half the feta, reserving the rest for garnish.

LIME SYRUP

2 limes

2 tablespoons granulated sugar

Squeeze the juice of the 2 limes into a small sauté pan and add the sugar. Cook over medium high heat until the sugar is dissolved, about 2 minutes.

Let the lime syrup cool. Then fold it into the watermelon salad. Place the salad in a bowl and garnish it with the remaining feta and fresh mint chiffonade. *Serves 20*

PHOTOGRAPH BY KEITH MCGRAW

❧ Green-Apple Tarte Tatin with Caramel Sauce

Apples are typically in season from August until spring, but Blake says the best time to use apples is from late September until early November. A green variety such as Granny Smith tends to be heartier and hold up to hotter temperatures. This recipe was invented by the Tatin sisters and introduced to Paris at Maxim's de Paris restaurant around the turn of the century. With few ingredients, it seems simple. Its elegance is in the execution.

DOUGH (PÂTE BRISÉE)

¾ cup all-purpose flour

¾ cup cake flour

¼ teaspoon salt

½ pound unsalted butter

½ cup ice-cold water

Flour for rolling out the dough

TARTE FILLING

6 tablespoons unsalted butter

¼ cup sugar

6 tart green apples such as Granny Smith, peeled and quartered with the cores removed, and each quarter cut in half again (set aside in water with a squeeze of lemon)

If you have a food processor, place all dry ingredients plus the butter in the bowl and pulse until you have little crumbled pea-sized pieces. Transfer these pieces to a mixing bowl. Sprinkle with ice water and bring the dough together with your hands. Don't over mix. Form the dough into a ball. Wrap it in plastic and refrigerate it for at least 2 hours.

If you don't have a food processor, place all the dry ingredients together with the butter in a mixing bowl and crumble the mixture with your fingers until it forms small pea-sized pieces. Proceed as above.

(CONTINUED)

TARTE FILLING

Place the unsalted butter and sugar in a 12-inch cast-iron skillet. Place over medium heat until the butter is melted. Do not overheat this mixture. Remove the skillet from the heat and place the apples in it, starting on the outside and shingling them around the circumference of the pan. Once you have completed the outside, start a second row inside the previous one and continue until the pan is full. You may have apple pieces left over; you should add these to the apples in the pan once they start cooking down.

Place the pan over medium heat. Notice where the butter starts to bubble in the pan first, and keep moving the skillet around to make sure all the apples are getting equal heat and cooking. As apples shrink you can add the remaining apples. Do not walk away from the stove during this step. You will have to adjust heat level several times and keep a close eye on the apples. If done right it, this step will take about 25–30 minutes. The apples will be done when you start to see caramel bubbling up around them.

Remove pan from heat.

CRUST

Preheat the oven to 375 degrees.

Sprinkle some flour on a sheet of parchment paper, and place the dough on the paper. Roll out the dough about ¼ inch thick to the approximate circumference of the skillet.

Dust any excess flour off the dough, slide it onto the apple filling, and tuck the dough into the sides. Be careful! Cast iron holds heat for a long time.

Place the tarte in the preheated oven for approximately 20 minutes or until the crust is golden brown.

Remove the tarte from the oven and let it sit for about 3 or 4 minutes. Place a serving plate over the pan and, using two pot holders, turn the tarte over. Let it sit upside down for a minute so all the apple filling will come out. Then lift off the skillet.

CARAMEL SAUCE

1 cup sugar

1 tablespoon corn syrup

¼ cup of water

½ cup heavy cream

2 tablespoons unsalted butter, softened

1 teaspoon vanilla extract

In a heavy sauce pan, over medium-high heat, stir together the sugar, corn syrup, and water. Heat these ingredients, stirring constantly, until the sugar dissolves and the syrup is bubbling. Stop stirring completely and allow the mixture to boil undisturbed until it turns a deep amber color. Immediately remove the pan from the heat. Slowly and carefully pour the heavy cream into the caramel. It will bubble up a lot. Use a high-temperature-resistant rubber spatula or wooden spoon to stir the mixture until smooth, scraping up the thicker part that settles on the bottom. If you have any lumps, just return the sauce to the heat to melt them. Stir in the butter. The sauce will be streaky, but it becomes more uniform after cooling slightly.

Stir in the vanilla extract. This recipe makes approximately 1 cup of caramel sauce.

Pour the caramel sauce over the tarte just before serving.

Serves 10–12

✺ Linzertorte Cookies

For a Christmas event one year, Blake suggested Linzertorte cookies. As it turns out, Harris loved these cookies as a child. When Blake heard that, he remarked: "I think about how fortunate I am to be able to do something that can take a person back to a specific moment in time, a fond memory. As a chef this is what I strive to do!"

Hazelnuts are classic in this recipe but are sometimes hard to find. You may substitute almonds.

⅔ cup hazelnuts or almonds

½ cup light-brown sugar, packed

2½ cups all-purpose flour

½ teaspoon baking powder

½ teaspoon salt

¼ teaspoon ground cinnamon

2 sticks unsalted butter, softened

1 large egg

1 teaspoon vanilla extract

Flour for dusting dough

1 cup confectionary sugar

1 12-ounce jar seedless
    raspberry jam

PHOTOGRAPH BY KEITH MCGRAW

Place the oven rack in the middle position and preheat to 350 degrees.

On a sheet pan, toast hazelnuts or almonds for about 6 minutes. Keep a close watch as they can overtoast in a matter of seconds. Cool the nuts to room temperature. If you use hazelnuts, put them in a clean kitchen towel and rub them to get rid of any loose skins. (Some may not come off.)

In a food processor, pulse the nuts with ¼ cup of the brown sugar until the nuts are finely ground.

In a small bowl whisk together the flour, baking powder, salt, and cinnamon.

Using an electric mixer, beat together the butter and the remaining ¼ cup of brown sugar at medium-high speed until pale and fluffy. This step will take about 3 minutes in a stand mixer fitted with a paddle attachment or 6 minutes with a hand-held mixer. Add the nut mixture and beat until all ingredients are well combined, about 1 minute. Beat in the egg and vanilla. Reduce the speed to low and add the flour mixture, mixing until just incorporated.

Using floured hands, form the dough into two balls. Flatten each into about a 5-inch disk. Wrap in plastic and chill for at least 2 hours.

Place the chilled dough on a piece of floured parchment paper. Flour the top of the dough and place another sheet of parchment on top, roll out each disk to a circle about 11 inches in circumference and about ⅛ inch thick. Using a brush, dust the extra flour off the top of the dough.

Cut out as many cookies as you can, using a 2-inch round cookie cutter. Transfer them to a parchment-lined sheet pan. Reroll the remaining dough only once. Using a small heart-shaped cookie cutter, cut the middle out of half the cookies. Bake all cookies for about 10 minutes or until the edges start turning golden.

Let the cookies cool completely.

Use the cookies that have their middles cut out for the tops of the sandwich-style Linzertortes. Dust these with an even, fairly heavy coat of confectionary sugar.

Spread the uncut cookies with about ½ inch of raspberry jam, then very gently place the top pieces of the cookies onto the jam, being careful not to smear the confectionary sugar.

Makes about 24–30 cookies

References

Allen, Katherine Thompson. *The University of South Carolina Horseshoe: Heart of the Campus* [brochure]. Edited by Elizabeth Cassidy West. Columbia: University of South Carolina Archives, University Libraries, University of South Carolina, n.d.

Ashley, Dottie. "President's House: Building on USC Horseshoe Is an Official Residence and More." *Columbia Record,* June 7, 1984.

At the University of South Carolina [brochure]. N.p, n.d. [Sorensen administration].

Brunton, Hal. *Renovation & Restoration of the USC Horseshoe: A Memoir.* Edited by Nancy Washington. Columbia: Caroline McKissick Dial Endowment, University of South Carolina, 2002.

Buildings of the Columbia Campus, the University of South Carolina: An Architectural and Historical Look at the Columbia Campus of the University of South Carolina. Columbia: Division of University Relations, 1990.

Edgar, Walter, and Norma Palms. "University of South Carolina President's House." Produced by Sandra Wertz. Unpublished draft of documentary script, SCETV, n.d.

Green, Edwin L. *History of the Buildings of the University of South Carolina.* Columbia: R. L. Bryan, 1909.

Heath, J. Cantey, Jr. "The University of South Carolina's Historic President's House." *Columbia Metropolitan Magazine.* January/February 1992.

The Horseshoe at the University of South Carolina [brochure]. N.p, n.d.

Information on the President's House and its furnishings compiled by house managers.

Institute for Southern Studies. *Remembering the Days: An Illustrated History of the University of South Carolina.* Columbia: R. L. Bryan, 1982.

Morby, Sarah J. "The House on the Horseshoe." Unpublished manuscript, 2000.

The President's House on the Historic Horseshoe [brochure]. N.p, n.d. [Palms administration].

Terry, George, "The President's House: University of South Carolina." Unpublished manuscript, circa 2001.

Washington, Nancy H. "At Home on the Horseshoe: The President's House at the University of South Carolina." Unpublished manuscript, circa 2002.

West, Elizabeth Cassidy. *The University of South Carolina.* Charleston: Arcadia, 2006.

West, Elizabeth Cassidy, and Katharine Thompson Allen. *On the Horseshoe: A Guide to the Historic Campus of the University of South Carolina.* Columbia: University of South Carolina Press, 2015.

Index

Page references given in *italics* indicate illustrations or material contained in their captions.